Modern Critical Interpretations

Sophocles'
Oedipus Rex

Modern Critical Interpretations

These and other titles in preparation

Modern Critical Interpretations

Sophocles'
Oedipus Rex

Edited and with an introduction by

Harold Bloom
Sterling Professor of the Humanities
Yale University

Chelsea House Publishers

NEW YORK ◇ PHILADELPHIA

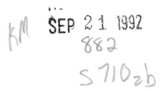
© 1988 by Chelsea House Publishers, a division
of Main Line Book Co.

Introduction © 1988 by Harold Bloom

Printed and bound in the United States of America

10 9 8 7 6 5 4

∞ The paper used in this publication meets the minimum
requirements of the American National Standard for Permanence
of Paper for Printed Library Materials, Z39.48–1984.

Library of Congress Cataloging-in-Publication Data
Sophocles' Oedipus Rex.
   (Modern critical interpretations)
   Bibliography: p.
   Includes index.
   Summary: A collection of eight critical essays
on the classical tragedy, arranged in chronological
order of their original publication.
   1. Sophocles. Oedipus Rex.   2. Oedipus (Greek
mythology) in literature. [1. Sophocles. Oedipus
Rex.   2. Oedipus (Greek mythology) in literature.
3. Classical literature—History and criticism]
I. Bloom, Harold. II. Series.
PA4413.07S66   1988   882'.01   87-9254
ISBN 0-87754-918-4

Contents

Editor's Note

This book brings together a representative selection of the best modern critical interpretations of the *Oedipus Rex* of Sophocles. The critical essays are reprinted here in the chronological order of their original publication. I am grateful to Douglas Smith for his erudite assistance.

My introduction centers upon the dialectic of innocence and ignorance in Oedipus, and upon his motives for self-blinding. Bernard Knox begins the chronological sequence with a meditation upon the relative stature of Oedipus and the Sophoclean gods. Dramatic intention and effect is the emphasis of John Jones, while E. R. Dodds, in a vigorous polemic, warns against various misunderstandings of the tragedy, which he implies has its crucial contrast in the struggle between the intelligence of Oedipus and the necessity for humans to live in illusions.

For Thomas Gould, taking issue with Dodds, Oedipus is essentially innocent, which places the blame on fate or the gods. Karl Reinhardt rejects all categories of innocence or guilt, and argues instead that the Sophoclean concern has to do with questions of illusion and truth.

In a study of the play's structure, J. P. Vernant emphasizes ambiguity as the crucial factor, an enigma that even heroic questioning can never resolve fully. That ambiguity is seen as a problem of language in the two final essays of this volume. Charles Segal asserts that the play is altogether about language, so that the riddle of the Sphinx becomes the problematic aspects of language itself. In a previously unpublished essay, the language of the hero, Oedipus, is studied by John Gould, who concludes strikingly that it gives a sense of the hero belonging not just among men but also to an alien cosmos that mocks our own. Oedipus and his fate finally make no sense in our world, because the story of Oedipus, in part, relies upon the language of the gods.

Introduction

Whether there is a "tragic flaw," a *hamartia,* in King Oedipus is uncertain, though I doubt it, as he is hardly a figure who shoots wide of the mark. Accuracy is implicit in his nature. We can be certain that he is free of that masterpiece of ambivalence—Freud's Oedipal complex. In the Age of Freud, we are unsure what to do with a guiltless Oedipus, but that does appear to be the condition of Sophocles' hero. We cannot read *Oedipus the King* as we read the *Iliad* of Homer, where the gods matter enormously. And even more, we know it is absurd to read *Oedipus* as though it were written by the Yahwist, or the authors of Jeremiah or Job, let alone of the Gospels. We can complete our obstacle course by warning ourselves not to compound *Oedipus* with *Hamlet* or *Lear.* Homer and the Bible, Shakespeare and Freud, teach us only how not to read Sophocles.

When I was younger, I was persuaded by Cedric Whitman's eloquent book on Sophocles to read *Oedipus* as a tragedy of "heroic humanism." I am not so persuaded now, not because I am less attracted by a humanistic heroism, but because I am uncertain how such a stance allows for tragedy. William Blake's humanism was more than heroic, being apocalyptic, but it too would not authorize tragedy. However the meaning of *Oedipus* is to be interpreted in our post-Nietzschean age, the play is surely tragedy, or the genre will lose coherence. E. R. Dodds, perhaps assimilating Sophocles to the *Iliad,* supposed that the tragedy of Oedipus honored the gods, without judging them to be benign or even just. Bernard Knox argues that the greatness of the gods and the greatness of Oedipus are irreconcilable, with tragedy the result of that schism. That reduces to the Hegelian view of tragedy as an agon between right and right, but Knox gives the preference to Oedipus, since the gods, being ever victorious, therefore cannot be heroic. A less Homeric reading than

1

Dodds's, this seems to me too much our sense of heroism—Malraux perhaps, rather than Sophocles.

Freud charmingly attributed to Sophocles, as a precursor of psychoanalysis, the ability to have made possible a self-analysis for the playgoer. But then Freud called *Oedipus* an "immoral play," since the gods ordained incest and patricide. Oedipus therefore participates in our universal unconscious sense of guilt, but on this reading so do the gods. I sometimes wish that Freud had turned to Aeschylus instead, and given us the Prometheus complex rather than the Oedipus complex. Plato is Oedipal in regard to Homer, but Sophocles is not. I hardly think that Sophocles would have chastised Homer for impiety, but then, as I read it, the tragedy of Oedipus takes up a more skeptical stance than that of Plato, unless one interprets Plato as Montaigne wished to interpret him.

What does any discerning reader remember most vividly about *Oedipus the King*? Almost certainly, the answer must be the scene of the king's self-blinding, as narrated by the second messenger, here in David Grene's version:

> You did not see the sight.
> Yet in so far as I remember it
> you'll hear the end of our unlucky queen.
> When she came raging into the house she went
> straight to her marriage bed, tearing her hair
> with both her hands, and crying upon Laius
> long dead—Do you remember, Laius,
> that night long past which bred a child for us
> to send you to your death and leave
> a mother making children with her son?
> And then she groaned and cursed the bed in which
> she brought forth husband by her husband, children
> by her own child, an infamous double bond.
> How after that she died I do not know,—
> for Oedipus distracted us from seeing.
> He burst upon us shouting and we looked
> to him as he paced frantically around,
> begging us always: Give me a sword, I say,
> to find this wife no wife, this mother's womb,
> this field of double sowing whence I sprang
> and where I sowed my children! As he raved

some god showed him the way—none of us there.
Bellowing terribly and led by some
invisible guide he rushed on the two doors,—
wrenching the hollow bolts out of their sockets,
he charged inside. There, there, we saw his wife
hanging, the twisted rope around her neck.
When he saw her, he cried out fearfully
and cut the dangling noose. Then, as she lay,
poor woman, on the ground, what happened after,
was terrible to see. He tore the brooches—
the gold chased brooches fastening her robe—
away from her and lifting them up high
dashed them on his own eyeballs, shrieking out
such things as: they will never see the crime
I have committed or had done upon me!
Dark eyes, now in the days to come look on
forbidden faces, do not recognize
those whom you long for—with such imprecations
he struck his eyes again and yet again
with the brooches. And the bleeding eyeballs gushed
and stained his beard—no sluggish oozing drops
but a black rain and bloody hail poured down.
So it has broken—and not on one head
but troubles mixed for husband and for wife.
The fortune of the days gone by was true
good fortune—but today groans and destruction
and death and shame—of all ills can be named
not one is missing.

(1.1238-86)

The scene, too terrible for acting out, seems also too dreadful for representation in language. Oedipus, desiring to put a sword in the womb of Jocasta, is led by "some god" to where he can break through the two doors (I shudder as I remember Walt Whitman's beautiful trope for watching a woman in childbirth, "I recline by the sills of the exquisite flexible doors"). Fortunately finding Jocasta self-slain, lest he add the crime of matricide to patricide and incest, Oedipus, repeatedly stabbing his eyes with Jocasta's brooches, passes judgment not so much upon seeing as upon the seen, and so upon the light by which we see. I interpret this as his protest against Apollo, who brings both the light and the plague. The Freudian trope of blinding for castration seems to me less relevant here than the outcry against the god.

To protest Apollo is necessarily dialectical, since the pride and agility of the intellect of Oedipus, remorselessly searching out the truth, in some sense is also Apollo's. That must mean that the complaint is also against the nature of truth. In this vision of reality, you shall know the truth, and the truth will make you mad. What would make Oedipus free? Nothing that happens in this play, must be the answer, nor does it seem that becoming an oracular god later on makes you free either. If you cannot be free of the gods, then you cannot be made free, and even acting as though your daemon is your destiny will not help you either.

The startling ignorance of Oedipus when the drama begins is the *given* of the play, and cannot be questioned or disallowed. Voltaire was scathing upon this, but the ignorance of the wise and the learned remains an ancient truth of psychology, and torments us every day. I surmise that this is the true force of Freud's Oedipus complex: not the unconscious sense of guilt, but the necessity of ignorance, lest the reality-principle destroy us. Nietzsche, rather than Freud, is the truest guide to *Oedipus the King*. We possess the highest art, the drama of Sophocles and of Shakespeare, lest we perish of the truth. That is not a Sophoclean irony, since Nietzsche said it not in praise of art, but so as to indicate the essential limitation of art. Sophoclean irony is more eloquent yet:

> CREON: Do not seek to be master in everything, for the
> things you mastered did not follow you throughout
> your life.
>
> *(As Creon and Oedipus go out.)*
>
> CHORUS: You that live in my ancestral Thebes, behold
> this Oedipus,—him who knew the famous riddles
> and was a man most masterful; not a citizen who
> did not look with envy on his lot—see him now
> and see the breakers of misfortune swallow him!
> Look upon that last day always. Count no mortal
> happy till he has passed the final limit of his life se-
> cure from pain.
>
> (1.1521–30)

Sophocles' Oedipus

Bernard Knox

Sophocles' Oedipus is not only the greatest creation of a major poet and the classic representative figure of his age: he is also one of the long series of tragic protagonists who stand as symbols of human aspiration and despair before the characteristic dilemma of Western civilization—the problem of man's true stature, his proper place in the universe.

In the earlier of the two Sophoclean plays which deal with the figure of Oedipus, this fundamental problem is raised at the very beginning of the prologue by the careful distinctions which the priest makes in defining his attitude toward Oedipus, the former savior of Thebes, its absolute ruler, and its last hope of rescue from the plague. "We beg your help," he says, "regarding you not as one equated to the gods, θεοῖσι . . . οὐκ ἰσούμενον, but as first of men."

"Not equated to the gods, but first of men." The positive part of the statement at any rate is undeniably true. Oedipus is *tyrannos* of Thebes, its despotic ruler. The Greek word corresponds neither to Shelley's "Tyrant" nor to Yeats's "King": tyrannos is an absolute ruler, who may be a bad ruler, or a good one (as Oedipus clearly is), but in either case he is a ruler who has seized power, not inherited it. He is not a king, for a king succeeds only by birth; the tyrannos succeeds by brains, force, influence. "This absolute power, τυραννίς," says Oedipus in the play "is a prize won with masses and money." This title of Oedipus, tyrannos, is one of the most pow-

From *Tragic Themes in Western Literature,* edited by Cleanth Brooks. © 1955 by Yale University. Yale University Press, 1955.

erful ironies of the play, for, although Oedipus does not know it, he is not only tyrannos, the outsider who came to power in Thebes, he is also the legitimate king by birth, for he was born the son of Laius. Only when his identity is revealed can he properly be called king: and the chorus refers to him by this title for the first time in the great ode which it sings after Oedipus knows the truth.

But the word tyrannos has a larger significance. Oedipus, to quote that same choral ode, is a παράδειγμα, a paradigm, an example to all men; and the fact that he is tyrannos, self-made ruler, the proverbial Greek example of worldly success won by individual intelligence and exertion, makes him an appropriate symbol of civilized man, who was beginning to believe, in the fifth century B.C., that he could seize control of his environment and make his own destiny, become, in fact, equated to the gods. "Oedipus shot his arrow far beyond the range of others"—the choral ode again—"and accomplished the conquest of complete prosperity and happiness."

Oedipus became tyrannos by answering the riddle of the Sphinx. It was no easy riddle, and he answered it, as he proudly asserts, without help from prophets, from bird-signs, from gods; he answered it alone, with his intelligence. The answer won him a city and the hand of a queen. And the answer to the Sphinx's riddle was— Man. In Sophocles' own century the same answer had been proposed to a great riddle. "Man," said Protagoras the sophist, "is the measure of all things."

Protagoras's famous statement is the epitome of the critical and optimistic spirit of the middle years of the fifth century; its implications are clear—man is the center of the universe, his intelligence can overcome all obstacles, he is master of his own destiny, tyrannos, self-made ruler who has the capacity to attain complete prosperity and happiness.

In an early Sophoclean play, Antigone, the chorus sings a hymn to this man the conqueror. "Many are the wonders and terrors, and nothing more wonderful and terrible than man." He has conquered the sea, "this creature goes beyond the white sea pressing forward as the swell crashes about him"; and he has conquered the land, "earth, highest of the gods . . . he wears away with the turning plough." He has mastered not only the elements, sea and land, but the birds, beasts, and fishes; "through knowledge and technique," sings the chorus, he is yoker of the horse, tamer of the bull. "And he has taught himself speech and thought swift as the wind and attitudes which enable him to live in communities and means to shelter himself from the frost and rain. Full of resources he faces the future, nothing will find him at a loss. Death, it is true, he will not avoid, yet he has thought out ways of escape from desperate diseases. His knowledge, ingenuity and technique are beyond anything that could have been foreseen." These lyrics describe the rise to power of *anthropos tyrannos;* self-taught he seizes control of his environment, he is master of the elements, the animals, the arts and sciences of civilization. "Full of resources he faces the future"—an apt description of Oedipus at the beginning of our play.

And it is not the only phrase of this ode which is relevant; for Oedipus is connected by the terms he uses, and which are used to and about him, with the whole range of human achievement and which has raised man to his present level. All the items of this triumphant catalogue recur in the *Oedipus Tyrannos;* the images of the play define him as helmsman, conqueror of the sea, and ploughman, conqueror of the land, as hunter, master of speech and thought, inventor, legislator, physician. Oedipus is faced in the play with an intellectual problem, and as he marshals his intellectual resources to solve it, the language of the play suggests a comparison between Oedipus's methods in the play and the whole range of sciences and techniques which have brought man to mastery, made him tyrannos of the world.

Oedipus's problem is apparently simple: "Who is the murderer of Laius?" but as he pursues the answer the question changes shape. It becomes a different problem: "Who am I?" And the answer to this problem involves the gods as well as the man. The answer to the question is not what he expected, it is in fact a reversal, that *peripeteia* which Aristotle speaks of in connection with this play. The state of Oedipus is reversed from "first of men" to "most accursed of men"; his attitude from the proud ἀρκτέον "I must rule" to the humble πειστέον, "I must obey." "Reversal" says Aristotle, "is a change of the action into the opposite," and one meaning of this much disputed phrase is that the action produces the opposite of the actor's intentions. So Oedipus curses the murderer of Laius and it turns out that he has cursed himself. But this reversal is not confined to the action; it is also the process of all the great images of the play which identify Oedipus as the inventive, critical spirit of his century. As the images unfold, the enquirer turns into the object of enquiry, the hunter into the prey, the doctor into the patient, the investigator into the criminal, the revealer into the thing revealed, the finder into the thing found, the savior into the thing saved ("I was saved, for some dreadful destiny"), the liberator into the thing released ("I released your feet from the bonds which pierced your ankles" says the Corinthian messenger), the accuser becomes the defendant, the ruler the subject, the teacher not only the pupil but also the object lesson, the example. A change of the action into its opposite, from active to passive.

And the two opening images of the Antigone ode recur with hideous effect. Oedipus the helmsman, who steers the ship of state, is seen, in Tiresias's words, as one who "steers his ship into a nameless anchorage," "who" in the chorus's words "shared the same great harbour with his father." And Oedipus the ploughman— "How," asks the chorus, "how could the furrows which your father ploughed bear you in silence for so long?"

This reversal is the movement of the play, parallel in the imagery and the action: it is the overthrow of the tyrannos, of man who seized power and thought himself "equated to the gods." The bold metaphor of the priest introduces another of the images which parallel in their development the reversal of the hero, and which suggest that Oedipus is a figure symbolic of human intelligence and achievement in general. He is not only helmsman, ploughman, inventor, legislator, liberator, revealer, doctor—he is also equator, mathematician, calculator; "equated" is a mathematical term, and it is only one of a whole complex of such terms which present Oedipus in yet a fresh aspect of man tyrannos. One of Oedipus's favorite words is "measure" and this is of course a significant metaphor: measure, mensuration, number, calculation—these are among the most important inventions which have brought man to power. Aeschylus's Prometheus, the mythical civilizer of human life, counts number among the foremost of his gifts to man. "And number, too, I invented, outstanding among clever devices." In the river valleys of the East generations of mensuration and calculation had brought man to an understanding of the movements of the stars and of time: in the histories of his friend Herodotus Sophocles had read of the calculation and mensuration which had gone into the building of the pyramids. "Measure"—it is Protagoras's word: "Man is the measure of all things." In this play man's measure is taken, his true equation found. The play is full of equations, some of them incomplete, some false; the final equation shows man equated not to the gods but to himself, as Oedipus is finally equated to himself. For there are in the play not one Oedipus but two.

One is the magnificent figure set before us in the opening scenes, tyrannos, the man of wealth and power, first of men, the intellect and energy which drives on the search. The other is the object of the search, a shadowy figure who has violated the most fundamental human taboos, an incestuous parricide, "most accursed of men." And even before the one Oedipus finds the other, they are connected and equated in the name which they both bear, Oedipus. Oedipus—Swollen-foot; it emphasizes the physical blemish which scars the body of the splendid tyrannos, a defect which he tries to forget but which reminds us of the outcast child this tyrannos once was and the outcast man he is soon to be. The second half of the name πούς, "foot," recurs throughout the play, as a mocking phrase which recalls this other Oedipus. "The Sphinx forced us to look at what was at our feet," says Creon. Tiresias invokes "the dread-footed curse of your father and mother." And the choral odes echo and re-echo with this word. "Let the murderer of Laius set his foot in motion in flight." "The murderer is a man alone with forlorn foot." "The laws of Zeus are high-footed." "The man of pride plunges down into doom where he cannot use his foot."

These mocking repetitions of one-half the name invoke the unknown Oedipus who will be revealed: the equally emphatic repetition of the first half emphasizes the dominant attitude of the man before us. Oidi—"swell," but it is also Oida, "I know," and this word is often, too often, in Oedipus's mouth. His knowledge is what makes him tyrannos, confident and decisive; knowledge has made man what he is, master of the world. Οἶδα, "I know"—it runs through the play with the same mocking persistence as πούς, "foot," and sometimes reaches an extreme of macabre punning emphasis.

When the messenger, to take one example of many, comes to tell Oedipus that his father, Polybus, is dead, he enquires for Oedipus, who is in the palace, in the following words:

> Strangers, from you might I learn where
> is the palace of the tyrannos Oedipus,
> best of all, where he is himself if you know where.

Here it is in the Greek:

ἆρ' ἄν παρ' ὑμῶν ὦ ξένοι μάθοιμ' ὅπου (oimopou)
τὰ τοῦ τυράννου δώματ' ἐστὶν Οἰδίπου (oidipou)
μάλιστα δ' αὐτὸν εἴπατ' εἰ κάτισθ' ὅπου (isthopou)

Those punning rhyming line-endings, μάθοιμ' ὅπου, Οἰδίπου, κάτισθ' ὅπου, "learn where," "Oedipus," "know where," unparalleled elsewhere in Greek tragedy, are a striking example of the boldness with which Sophocles uses language: from the "sweet singer of Colonus" they are somewhat unexpected, they might almost have been written by the not-so-sweet singer of Trieste-Zürich-Paris.

Οἶδα, the knowledge of the tyrannos, πούς, the swollen foot of Laius's son—in the hero's name the basic equation is already symbolically present, the equation which Oedipus will finally solve. But the priest in the prologue is speaking of a different equation, ἰσούμενον, "We beg your help, not as one equated to the gods." It is a warning, and the warning is needed. For although Oedipus in the opening scenes is a model of formal and verbal piety, the piety is skin-deep. And even before he declares his true religion, he can address the chorus, which has been praying to the gods, with godlike words. "What you pray for you will receive, if you will listen to and accept what I am about to say."

The priest goes on to suggest a better equation: he asks Oedipus to equate himself to the man he was when he saved Thebes from the Sphinx. "You saved us then, be now the equal of the man you were." This is the first statement of the theme, the double Oedipus; here there is a contrast implied between the present Oedipus who is failing to save his city from the plague and the successful Oedipus of the past who answered the riddle of the Sphinx. He must answer a riddle again, be his old self, but the answer to this riddle will not be as simple as the answer to the first. When it is found, he will be equated, not to the foreigner who saved the city and became tyrannos, but to the native-born king, the son of Laius and Jocasta.

Oedipus repeats the significant word, "equal," ὅστις ἐξ ἴσου νοσεῖ. "Sick as you are, not one of you has sickness equal to mine," and he adds a word of his own, his characteristic metaphor. He is impatient at Creon's absence. "Measuring the day against the time (ξυμμετρούμενον χρόνῳ), I am worried." And then as Creon approaches, "He is now commensurate with the range of our voices."—ξύμμετρος γὰρ ὡς κλύειν.

Here is Oedipus the equator and measurer, this is the method by which he will reach the truth: calculation of time and place, measurement and comparison of age and number and description—these are the techniques which will solve the equation, establish the identity of the murderer of Laius. The tightly organized and relentless process by which Oedipus finds his way to the truth is the operation of the human intellect in many aspects; it is the investigation of the officer of the law who identifies the criminal, the series of diagnoses of the physician who identifies the disease—it has even been compared by Freud to the process of psychoanalysis—and it is also the working out of a mathematical problem which will end with the establishment of a true equation.

The numerical nature of the problem is emphasized at once with Creon's entry. "One man of Laius's party escaped," says Creon, "he had only one thing to say." "What is it?" asks Oedipus. "One thing might find a way to learn many." The one thing is that Laius was killed not by one man but by many. This sounds like a problem in arithmetic, and Oedipus undertakes to solve it. But the chorus which now comes on stage has no such confidence: it sings of the plague with despair, but it makes this statement in terms of the same metaphor; it has its characteristic word which, like the priest and like Oedipus, it pronounces twice. The chorus's word is ἀνάριθμος, "numberless," "uncountable." "My sorrows are beyond the count of number," and later, "uncountable the deaths of which the city is dying." The plague is something beyond the power of "number . . . outstanding among clever devices."

The prologue and the first stasimon, besides presenting the customary exposition of the plot, present also the exposition of the metaphor. And with the entry of Tiresias, the development of the metaphor begins, its terrible potentialities are revealed. "Even though you are tyrannos," says the prophet at the height of his anger, "you and I must be made equal in one thing, at least, the chance for an equal reply," ἐξισωτέον τὸ γοῦν ἴσ' ἀντιλέξαι. Tiresias is blind, and Oedipus will be made equal to him in this before the play is over. But there is more still. "There is a mass of evil of which you are unconscious which shall equate you to yourself and your children."

ἃ σ' ἐξισώσει σοί τε καὶ τοῖς σοῖς τέκνοις.

This is not the equation the priest desired to see, Oedipus present equated with Oedipus past, the deliverer from the Sphinx, but a more terrible equation reaching farther back into the past, Oedipus son of Polybus and Merope equated to Oedipus son of Laius and Jocasta; "equate you with your own children," for Oedipus is the brother of his own sons and daughters. In his closing words Tiresias explains this mysterious line, and connects it with the unknown murderer of Laius. "He will be revealed, a native Theban, one who in his relationship with his own children is both brother and father, with his mother both son and husband, with his father, both marriage-partner and murderer. Go inside and reckon this up, λογίζου, and if you find me mistaken in my reckoning, ἐψευσμένον, then say I have no head for prophecy."

Tiresias adopts the terms of Oedipus's own science and throws them in his face. But these new equations are beyond Oedipus's understanding, he dismisses them as the ravings of an unsuccessful conspirator with his back to the wall. Even the chorus, though disturbed, rejects the prophet's words and resolves to stand by Oedipus.

After Tiresias, Creon: after the prophet, the politician. In Tiresias, Oedipus faced a blind man who saw with unearthly sight; but Creon's vision, like that of Oedipus, is of this world. They are two of a kind, and Creon talks Oedipus's language. It is a quarrel between two calculators. "Hear an equal reply," says Creon, and "Long time might be measured since Laius's murder." "You and Jocasta rule in equality of power." And finally "Am I not a third party equated, ἰσοῦμαι, to you two?" Creon and Oedipus are not equal now, for Creon is at the mercy of Oedipus, begging for a hearing; but before the play is over Oedipus will be at the mercy of Creon, begging kindness for his daughters, and he then uses the same word. "Do not equate them with my misfortunes."

μηδ' ἐξισώσῃς τάσδε τοῖς ἐμοῖς κακοῖς

With Jocasta's intervention the enquiry changes direction. In her attempt to comfort Oedipus, whose only accuser is a prophet, she indicts prophecy in general, using as an example the unfulfilled prophecy about her own child, who was supposed to kill Laius. The child was abandoned on the mountain-side and Laius was killed by robbers where three wagon roads meet. "Such were the definitions, διώρισαν, made by prophetic voices," and they were incorrect. But Oedipus is not, for the moment, interested in prophetic voices. "Where three wagon roads meet." He once killed a man at such a place and now in a series of swift questions he determines the relation of these two events. The place, the time, the description of the victim, the number in his party, five, all correspond exactly. His account of the circumstances includes Apollo's prophecy that he would kill his father and be his mother's mate. But this does not disturb him now. That prophecy has not been fulfilled, for his father and mother are in Corinth, where he will never go again. "I measure the distance to Corinth by the stars," ἄστροις . . . . ἐκμετρούμενος. What does disturb him is that he may be the murderer of Laius, the cause of the plague, the object of his own solemn excommunication. But he has some slight ground for hope. There is a discrepancy in the two events. It is the same numerical distinction which was discussed before, whether Laius was killed by one man or many. Jocasta said robbers and Oedipus was alone. This distinction is now all-important, the key to the solution of the equation. Oedipus sends for the survivor who can confirm or deny the saving detail. "If he says the same number as you then I am not the murderer. For one cannot equal many."

 οὐ γὰε γένοιτ' ἂν εἷς γε τοῖς πολλοῖς ἴσος

which may fairly be rendered, "In no circumstances can one be equal to more than one." Oedipus's guilt or innocence rests now on a mathematical axiom.

But a more fundamental equation has been brought into question, the relation of the oracles to reality. Here are two oracles, both the same, both unfulfilled; the same terrible destiny was predicted for Jocasta's son, who is dead, and for Oedipus, who has avoided it. One thing is clear to Jocasta. Whoever turns out to be Laius's murderer, the oracles are wrong. "From this day forward I would not, for all prophecy can say, turn my head this way or that." If the equation of the oracles with reality is a false equation, then religion is meaningless. Neither Jocasta nor Oedipus can allow the possibility that the oracles are right, and they accept the consequences, as they proceed to make clear. But the chorus cannot, and it now abandons Oedipus the calculator and turns instead to those "high-footed laws, which are the children of Olympus and not a creation of mortal man." It calls on Zeus to fulfill the oracles. "If these things do not coincide," ἁρμόσει, if the oracles do not equal reality, then "the divine order is overthrown," ἔρρει τὰ θεῖα. The situation and future of two individuals has become a test of divine power: if they are right, sings the chorus, "why reverence Apollo's Delphi, the center of the world? Why join the choral dance?" τί δεῖ με χορεύειν; and with this phrase the issue is brought out of the past into the present moment in the theater of Dionysus. For this song itself is also a dance, the choral stasimon which is the nucleus of tragedy and which reminds us that tragedy itself is an act of religious worship. If the oracles and the truth are not equated the performance of the play has no meaning, for tragedy is a religious ritual. This phrase is a tour de force which makes the validity of the performance itself depend on the dénouement of the play.

The oracles are now the central issue; the murder of Laius fades into the background. A messenger from Corinth brings news, news which will be greeted, he announces, "with an equal amount of sorrow and joy." "What is it," asks Jocasta, "which has such double power?" Polybus is dead. The sorrow equal to the joy will come later; for the moment there is only joy. The oracles are proved wrong again: Oedipus's father is dead. Oedipus can no more kill his father than the son of Laius killed his. "Oracles of the gods, where are you now?" Oedipus is caught up in Jocasta's exaltation, but it does not last. Only half his burden has been lifted from him. His mother still lives. He must still measure the distance to Corinth by the stars, still fear the future.

Both Jocasta and the messenger now try to relieve him of this last remaining fear. Jocasta makes her famous declaration in which she rejects fear, providence, divine and human alike, and indeed any idea of order or plan. Her declaration amounts almost to a rejection of the law of cause and effect: and it certainly attacks the basis of human calculation. For her, the calculation has gone far enough: it has produced an acceptable result; let it stop here. "Why should man fear?" she asks. "His life is governed by the operation of chance. Nothing can be accurately foreseen. The best rule is to live blindly, at random, εἰκῇ, as best one can." It is a statement which recognizes and accepts a meaningless universe. And Oedipus would agree, but for one thing. His mother lives. He must still fear.

Where Jocasta failed the messenger succeeds. He does it by destroying the equation on which Oedipus's life is based. And he uses familiar terms. "Polybus is no more your father than I, but equally so." Oedipus's question is indignant: "How can my father be equal to a nobody, a zero? τῷ μηδενί" The answer—"Polybus is not your father, neither am I." But that is as far as the Corinthian's knowledge goes; he was given the child Oedipus by another, a shepherd, one of Laius's men. And now the two separate equations begin to merge. "I think," says the chorus, "that that shepherd was the same man that you already sent for." The eyewitness to the death of Laius. He was sent for to say whether Laius was killed by one or many, but he will bring more important news. He will finally lift from Oedipus's shoulders the burden of fear he has carried since he left Delphi. Chance governs all. Oedipus's life history is the operation of chance; found by one shepherd, passed on to another, given to Polybus who was childless, brought up as heir to a kingdom, self-exiled from Corinth he came to Thebes a homeless wanderer, answered the riddle of the Sphinx, and won a city and the hand of a queen. And that same guiding chance will now reveal to him his real identity. Jocasta was right. Why should he fear?

But Jocasta has already seen the truth. Not chance, but the fulfillment of the oracle; the prophecy and the facts coincide (ἁρμόσει), as the chorus prayed they would. Jocasta is lost, but she tries to save Oedipus, to stop the enquiry. But nothing can stop him now. Her farewell to him expresses her agony and knowledge by its omissions: she recognizes but cannot formulate the dreadful equation which Tiresias stated, "ἰού, ἰού, δύστηνε, Unfortunate. This is the only name I can call you." She cannot call him husband. The three-day-old child she sent out to die on the mountainside has been restored to her, and she cannot call him son.

Oedipus hardly listens. He in his turn has scaled the same heights of confidence from which she has toppled, and he goes higher still. "I will know my origin, burst forth what will." He knows that it will be good. Chance governs the universe and Oedipus is her son. Not the son of Polybus, nor of any mortal man but the son of fortunate chance. In his exaltation he rises in imagination above human stature. "The months, my brothers, have defined, διώρισαν, my greatness and smallness"; he has waned and waxed like the moon, he is one of the forces of the universe, his family is time and space. It is a religious, a mystical conception; here is Oedipus's real religion, he is equal to the gods, the son of chance, the only real goddess. Why should he not establish his identity?

The solution is only a few steps ahead. The shepherd is brought on. "If I, who never met the man, may make an estimate (σταθμᾶσθαι), I think this is the shepherd who has been the object of our investigation (ζητοῦμεν). In age he is commensurate σύμμετρος with the Corinthian here." With this significant prologue he plunges into the final calculation.

The movement of the next sixty lines is the swift ease of the last stages of the mathematical proof: the end is half foreseen, the process an automatic sequence from one step to the next until Oedipus tyrannos and Oedipus the accursed, the knowledge and the swollen foot, are equated. "It all comes out clear," he cries. τὰ πάντ᾽ ἂν ἐξήκοι σαφῆς. The prophecy has been fulfilled. Oedipus knows himself for what he is. He is not the measurer but the thing measured, not the equator but the thing equated. He is the answer to the problem he tried to solve. The chorus sees in Oedipus a παράδειγμα, an example to mankind. In this self-recognition of Oedipus, man recognizes himself. Man measures himself and the result is not that man is the measure of all things. The chorus, which rejected number and all that it stood for, has learned to count; and states the result of the great calculation. "Generations of man that must die, I add up the total of your life and find it equal to zero." ἴσα καὶ τὸ μηδὲν ζώσας ἐναριθμῶ.

The overthrow of the tyrannos is complete. When Oedipus returns from the palace he is blind, and, by the terms of his own proclamation, an outcast. It is a terrible reversal, and it raises the question, "Is it deserved? How far is he responsible for what he has done? Were the actions for which he is now paying not predestined?" No. They were committed in ignorance, but they were not predestined, merely predicted. An essential distinction, as essential for Milton's Adam as for Sophocles' Oedipus. His will was free, his actions his own, but the pattern of his action is the same as that of the Delphic prophecy. The relation between the prophecy and Oedipus's actions is not that of cause and effect. It is the relation suggested by the metaphor, the relation of two independent entities which are equated.

Yet no man can look on Oedipus without sympathy. In his moment of exaltation—"I am the son of fortune"—he is man at his blindest, but he is also man at his most courageous and heroic: "Burst forth what will, I will know." And he has served, as the chorus says, to point a moral. He is a paradigm, a demonstration. True, Oedipus, the independent being, was a perfectly appropriate subject for the demonstration. But we cannot help feeling that the gods owe Oedipus a debt. Sophocles felt it too, and in his last years wrote the play which shows us the nature of the payment, *Oedipus at Colonus*.

This play deals with Oedipus's reward, and the reward is a strange one. How strange can be seen clearly if we compare Oedipus with another great figure who also served as the subject of a divine demonstration, Job. After his torment Job had it all made up to him. "The Lord gave Job twice as much as he had before. For he had 14,000 sheep, and 6,000 camels and 1,000 yoke of oxen and 1,000 she-asses. He had also 7 sons and 3 daughters. And after this lived Job an hundred and forty years, and saw his sons and his sons' sons, even four generations." This is the kind of reward we can under-stand—14,000 sheep, 6,000 camels—Job, to use an irreverent com-parison, hit the patriarchal jackpot. Oedipus's reward includes no camels or she-asses, no long life, in fact no life at all; his reward is death. But a death which Job could never imagine. For in death Oedipus becomes equated to the gods. The ironic phrase with which the first play began has here a literal fulfillment. Oedipus becomes something superhuman, a spirit which lives on in power in the affairs of men after the death of the body. His tomb is to be a holy place, for the city in whose territory his body lies will win a great victory on the field where Oedipus lies buried. By his choice of a burial place he thus influences history, becomes a presence to be feared by some and thanked by others. But it is not only in his grave that he will be powerful. In the last hours of his life he begins to assume the at-tributes of the divinity he is to become; the second play, *Oedipus at Colonus,* puts on stage the process of Oedipus's transition from hu-man to divine.

"Equated to the gods." We have not seen the gods, but we know from the first play what they are. That play demonstrated that the gods have knowledge, full complete knowledge, the knowledge which Oedipus thought he had. He was proved ignorant; real knowledge is what distinguishes god from man. Since the gods have knowledge their action is confident and sure. They act with the swift decision which was characteristic of Oedipus but which was in him misplaced. Only a god can be sure, not a man. And their action is just. It is a justice based on perfect knowledge, is exact and appro-priate, and therefore allows no room for forgiveness—but it can be angry. The gods can even mock the wrongdoer as Athene does Ajax, as the echoes of his name mocked Oedipus. This sure, full, angry justice is what Oedipus tried to administer to Tiresias, to Creon, but his justice was based on ignorance was injustice. These attributes of divinity—knowledge, certainty, justice—are the qualities Oedipus thought he possessed—and that is why he was the perfect example of the inadequacy of human knowledge, certainty, and justice. But in the second play Oedipus is made equal to the gods, he assumes the attributes of divinity, the attributes he once thought his, he becomes what he once thought he was. This old Oedipus seems to be equal to the young, confident in his knowledge, fiercely angry in his administration of justice, utterly sure of himself—but this time he is justified. These are not the proper attitudes for a man, but Oedipus is turning into something more than man; now he knows surely, sees clearly, the gods give Oedipus back his eyes, but they are eyes of superhuman vision. Now in his transformation, as then, in his reversal, he serves still as an example. The rebirth of the young, confident Oedipus in the tired old man emphasizes the same lesson; it defines once more the limits of man and the power of gods, states again that the possession of knowledge, certainty, and justice is what distinguishes god from man.

The opening statement of Oedipus shows that as a man he has learned the lesson well. "I have learned acquiescence, taught by suffering and long time." As a man Oedipus has nothing more to learn. With this statement he comes to the end of a long road. The nearby city whose walls he cannot see is Athens, and here is the place of his reward, his grave, his home. The welcome he receives is to be ordered off by the first arrival; he has trespassed on holy ground, the grove of the Eumenides. He knows what this means, this is the resting place he was promised by Apollo, and he refuses to move. His statement recalls the tyrannos, a characteristic phrase: "In no circumstances will I leave this place." The terms of his prayer to the goddesses of the grave foreshadow his transition from body to spirit. "Pity this wretched ghost of Oedipus the man, this body that is not what it once was long ago."

As a body, as a man, he is a thing to be pitied; he is blind, feeble, ragged, dirty. But the transformation has already begun. The first comer spoke to him with pity, even condescension, but the chorus of citizens which now enters feels fear. "Dreadful to see, dreadful to hear." When they know his identity their fear changes to anger, but Oedipus defends his past. He sees himself as one who was ignorant, who suffered rather than acted. But now he is actor, not sufferer. He comes with knowledge, and power. "I come bringing advantage to this city."

He does not yet know what advantage. His daughter Ismene

comes to tell him what it is, that his grave will be the site of a victory for the city that shelters him. And to tell him that his sons and Creon, all of whom despised and rejected him, now need him, and will come to beg his help. Oedipus has power over the future and can now reward his friends and punish his enemies. He chooses to reward Athens, to punish Creon and his own sons. He expresses his choice in terms which show a recognition of human limitations; Athens' reward, something which lies within his will, as an intention; his sons' punishment, something over which he has no sure control, as a wish. "May the issue of the battle between them lie in my hands. If that were to be, the one would not remain king, nor the other win the throne."

Theseus, the king of Athens, welcomes him generously, but when he learns that Thebes wants Oedipus back and that he refuses to go, Thesus reproaches the old man. "Anger is not what your misfortune calls for." And the answer is a fiery rebuke from a superior. "Wait till you hear what I say, before you reproach me." Oedipus tells Theseus that he will bring victory over Thebes at some future time, and Theseus, the statesman, is confident that Athens will never be at war with Thebes. Oedipus reproaches him in his turn. Such confidence is misplaced. No man should be so sure of the future: "Only to the gods comes no old age or death. Everything else is dissolved by all-powerful time. The earth's strength decays, the body decays, faith dies, mistrust flowers and the wind of friendship changes between man and man, city and city." No man can be confident of the future. Man's knowledge is ignorance. It is the lesson Oedipus learned in his own person and he reads it to Theseus now with all the authority of his blind eyes and dreadful name—but he does not apply it to himself. For he goes on to predict the future. He hands down the law of human behavior to Theseus speaking already as a *daemon,* not one subject to the law but one who administers it. And with his confident prediction, his assumption of sure knowledge, goes anger, but not the old human anger of Oedipus tyrannos. As he speaks of Thebes's future defeat on the soil where he will be buried, the words take on an unearthly quality, a daemonic wrath.

ἵν' οὑμὸς εὕδων καὶ κεκρυμμένος νεκύς
ψυχρὸς ποτ' αὐτῶν θερμὸν αἷμα πίεται
εἰ Ζεὺς ἔτι Ζεὺς χὠ Διὸς Φοῖβος σαφής.

"There my sleeping and hidden corpse, cold though it be, will drink their warm blood, if Zeus is still Zeus and Apollo a true prophet." What before was wish and prayer is now prediction. But the prediction is qualified: "if Apollo be a true prophet." He does not yet speak in the authority of his own name. That will be the final stage.

And when it comes, he speaks face to face with the objects of his anger. Creon's condescending and hypocritical speech is met with a blast of fury that surpasses the anger he had to face long ago in Thebes. The final interview is a repetition of the first. In both Creon is condemned, in both with the same swift vindictive wrath, but this time the condemnation is just. Oedipus sees through to the heart of Creon, he knows what he is: and Creon proceeds to show the justice of Oedipus's rejection by revealing that he has already kidnapped Ismene, by kidnapping Antigone, and laying hands on Oedipus himself. Oedipus is helpless, and only the arrival of Theseus saves him. This is the man who is being equated to the gods, not the splendid tyrannos, the man of power, vigor, strength, but a blind old man, the extreme of physical weakness, who cannot even see, much less prevent, the violence that is done him.

Physical weakness, but a new height of spiritual strength. This Oedipus judges justly and exactly, knows fully, sees clearly—his power is power over the future, the defeat of Thebes, the death of his sons, the terrible reversal of Creon. One thing Creon says to Oedipus clarifies the nature of the process we are witnessing. "Has not time taught you wisdom?" Creon expected to find the Oedipus of the opening scene of the play, whom time had taught acquiescence, but he finds what seems to be the tyrannos he knew and feared. "You harm yourself now as you did then," he says, "giving way to that anger which has always been your defeat." He sees the old Oedipus as equal to the young. In one sense they are, but in a greater sense they are no more equal than man is equal to the gods.

With the next scene the whole story comes full circle. A suppliant begs Oedipus for help. Our last sight of Oedipus is like our first. This suppliant is Polynices, his son, and the comparison with the opening scene of the first play is emphasized by the repetitions of the priest's speech—words, phrases, even whole lines—which appear in Polynices' appeal to his father. It is a hypocritical speech which needs no refutation. It is met with a terrible indictment which sweeps from accusation through prophecy to a climax which, with its tightly packed explosive consonants resembles not so much human speech as a burst of daemonic anger:

θανεῖν κτανεῖν θ᾽ὑφ᾽ οὗπερ ἐξελήλασαι
τοιαῦτ᾽ ἀρῶμαι καὶ καλῶ τὸ Ταρτάρου
στυγνὸν πατρῷον ἔρεβος ὡς σ᾽ἀποικίσῃ

"Kill and be killed by the brother who drove you out. This is my curse, I call on the hideous darkness of Tartarus where your fathers lie, to prepare a place for you." This is a superhuman anger welling from the outraged sense of justice not of a man but of the forces of the universe themselves.

Creon could still argue and resist, but to this speech no reply is possible. There can be no doubt of its authority. When Polynices discusses the speech with his sisters, the right word for it is found. Oedipus speaks with the voice of an oracle. "Will you go to Thebes and fulfill his prophecies? (μαντεύματα)" says Antigone. Oedipus who fought to disprove an oracle has become one himself. And his son now starts on the same road his father trod. "Let him prophecy. I do not have to fulfill it." Polynices leaves with a phrase that repeats his mother's denunciation of prophets. "All this is in the power of the divinity ἐν τῷ δαίμονι, it may turn out this way or that." In the power of a god—in the power of chance—whatever he means, he does not realize the sense in which the words are true. The daemon, the divinity, in whose power it lies is Oedipus himself.

Oedipus has stayed too long. Power such as this should not walk the earth in the shape of a man. The thunder and lightning summon him, and the gods reproach him for his delay. "You Oedipus, you, why do we hesitate to go? You have delayed too long."

ὦ οὗτος οὗτος Οἰδίπους τί μέλλομεν
χωρεῖν; πάλαι δὴ τἀπὸ σοῦ βραδύνεται.

These strange words are the only thing the gods say in either play. And as was to be expected of so long delayed and awful a statement, it is complete and final. The hesitation for which they reproach Oedipus is the last shred of his humanity, which he must now cast off. Where he is going vision is clear, knowledge certain, action instantaneous and effective; between the intention and the act there falls no shadow of hesitation or delay. The divine "we"—"Why do *we* hesitate to go"—completes and transcends the equation of Oedipus with the gods; his identity is merged with theirs. And in this last moment of his bodily life they call him by his name, *Oidipous,* the name which contains in itself the lesson of which not only his action and suffering but also his apotheosis serve as the great example— *oida*—that man's knowledge, which makes him master of the world, should never allow him to think that he is equated to the gods, should never allow him to forget the foot, *pous,* the reminder of his true measurement, his real identity.

Action and Actors

John Jones

It has been said that *Oedipus the King* possesses the merits of a good
detective story. The point of the comparison is not merely the piece-
meal disclosure of hidden facts, nor the process of investigation, but
a kind of mental innocence; Sophocles unfolds a cat-and-mouse situation of great horror while leaving the obvious psychological resources of anguish and dread and recurring false hopes strangely
unexploited. This suggests such highly stylised modern forms as the
detective story and the cowboy film where, because of a withdrawal
of human interest which leaves the action naked, we witness death
and pain lightheartedly.

But the comparison ends there, on the threshold of the
Sophoclean play's seriousness. This seriousness is hard to experience
since action's proper wealth of meaning for the fifth-century Greek
is virtually irrecoverable: to say that *Oedipus the King* is like a good
detective story is to suggest that the cat-and-mouse horrors are not
there at all, when in fact they rest in the action: the interrogations by
which Oedipus exposes the truth about himself have a sublime im-
personal malignity such as a series of forced moves at chess would
impart if the game possessed tragic relevance to life. Furthermore, to
say that *Oedipus the King* is like a good detective story is to ignore the
differentiation of action and plot upon which the *Poetics* depends.
Aristotle's intellectualist vision of the lucid form which the artist
coaxes out of rough circumstance must not be directly imposed on

From *On Aristotle and Greek Tragedy*. © 1962 by John Jones. Chatto & Windus Ltd.,
1962.

Sophocles, of course; but still a general correspondence exists between the Aristotelian form and that life-situation from myth which Sophocles' play defines and redefines, compresses, reduces, renders essentially, epitomoses. "He shall be found"—so the blind seer Teiresias declares—"at once brother and father to the children of his house, son and husband to the woman who bore him, murderer of his father and successor to his father's bed." Teiresias is a prophet; he speaks for the god and his words disclose the hard bedrock truth of the situation. The vulgar notion of prophecy as the power to predict future events must be absorbed within a wider and juster conception of god-inspired exposure of the myth's essentials; otherwise we fail to give due prominence to the fact (vital to the religious ambience of *Oedipus the King*) that the stage figures groping forward in the play's action are brought sharply up against something that was there before.

As the dreadful truth unfolds, the people in the play recall the terms of Teiresias' prophecy—with very striking iteration, but without pointed reference to the seer himself; they are falling upon the truth, only in a very secondary sense confirming a prediction, and we should place their mortal encounter with this adamantine quasi-substance in a context of the "Great Time" investing Sophoclean humanity, and of life's cruel margin which is called Necessity. And so they nurse the essential facts with strange unmorbid concentration. A messenger describes how Queen Jocasta, on the point of suicide, "bewailed the marriage in which, unhappy lady, she had borne a twofold race—husband by husband, children by her child"; and how Oedipus burst into the palace, asking "where he should find the wife that was no wife, but a mother who had borne his children and himself."

The same concentration is maintained by the newly blind Oedipus:

> Those three roads, that secret valley, that wood and narrow passage where the roads met and where I spilt—for the dust to drink up—my father's blood, and mine. . . . That marriage which gave me life, then gave life to other children from my seed; and created an incestuous kindred of fathers, brothers, sons, brides, wives, mothers.

He summons his young daughters to him:

> Where are you, my children? Come here—come to your brother's hands . . . which are the hands of a man who,

> seeing nothing, understanding nothing, became your fa-
> ther by her that bore him.

He contemplates the wretched life in store for them:

> What misery is lacking? Your father killed his father and
> got children by his mother, and you two are the fruit of the
> womb which once held him—

this series of declarations culminating in the demonstrative choral
gesture ("Behold, citizens of Thebes—this is Oedipus") with which
the play ends, and which the Chorus have themselves anticipated:

> Alas, renowned Oedipus! The one ample haven enfolded
> son and father; coming to your bride you found your own
> beginning. How was it, unhappy one, that the furrow
> which had received your father's seed received yours also
> without mark of protest, all this time?

Such definitional fondling of the truth, so far from being mor-
bid, is the means to restoration, and almost an act of peace. When
Sophocles' text has been given a fair hearing we respond to the
cooperative endeavour of the outward-turning masks in their advance towards full discovery of Oedipus. Our experience is of something decisively accomplished.

The play opens with the city of Thebes prostrate in a passion of
despair because of a mysterious pestilence or blight which is destroying its citizens and all living things there. A group of suppliants has
assembled to ask Oedipus to save the city. They approach him not
merely because he is their king but also because he saved Thebes once
before, when the monstrous Sphinx was oppressing her, and they
naturally turn to him now. Great stress is laid on Oedipus's fame and
proven virtuosity as a problem-solver; his finding the answer to the
Sphinx's riddle after all others had failed is repeatedly cited as a
reason for believing that he will again rescue the city. His task is to
find out what has angered heaven to the point of visiting Thebes
with pestilence, and then to make amends; and this task he success-
fully performs. This last point (which has been almost totally ignored) is very relevant to the final sense of accomplishment. Thebes
is put right with her gods, and the religious institutions of oracle and
prophecy are vindicated.

Oedipus's first step towards saving the city is to send Creon, his wife's brother, to consult the oracle of Apollo. On his carefully staged return Creon's first words are that he brings good news; the god declares that their troubles will end when they detect and punish the murderer of Laius, who was king of Thebes before Oedipus and died at the hands of an unknown assailant when on his way to Delphi. Their present sufferings are due to the defilement they have incurred by unwittingly harbouring the murderer.

And so the search begins. Of course, there is irony in the long struggle to reach the truth, and especially in the successful outcome; but it is an irony whose force and tone will be misapprehended so long as all judgment of the play is required to come to terms with the hero's tragic fate, making the play's meaning and message primarily those which it has for him, or even in relation to him as an independent dramatic *exemplum*. Oedipus's solitary eminence, which is undeniably dominant and impressive always, may be rendered in the critical language of Character and psychological individuation (isolating Oedipus by way of the pains and problems that assault the hero's consciousness), or of action: in the latter case we say that Oedipus stands alone because of the extent—unique in Greek drama— to which he carries the action single-handed. The true Sophoclean standpoint is suggested by a glancing reference in the *Antigone* to Oedipus's "sins brought to light by his own search"; Oedipus does the work in this success story, and *Oedipus the King* maintains throughout an extraordinary intimacy between the substantive sins themselves—their religio-moral quality, the subjective innocence of the wrongdoing and adjacent themes—and the sinner's action in laying them bare. A kind of godly faithfulness is lent to Oedipus's exertions by the fact that his progressive self-exposure is suspended in a mesh of oracle and prophecy; in fact it *is* the movement of these god-inspired pronouncements towards fulfilment, and its accomplishment *is* their final vindication. The process and its completion matter supremely.

We have noted Teiresias's words and the answer with which Creon returned from Delphi. Another and deeper oracular layer is exposed by the Chorus:

> I will go no more to Apollo's inviolate shrine at the navel
> of the world, nor to the temple at Abae, nor to Olympia,
> if these oracles fail in fulfilment so that each man's finger

points at them. . . . The old prophecies about Laius are losing their power; already men are dismissing them from mind, and Apollo is nowhere glorified with honours. Religion is dying.

They are referring to an earlier oracle or oracles which Laius received from Apollo's ministers at Delphi. Jocasta has already stated their content which was that Laius would one day be killed by the child of his marriage with herself. The reason for the Chorus's dismay is that these oracles appear to be utterly discredited; Jocasta's baby died at birth (as everyone supposes), and when Laius finally came to be murdered the accepted story was that "foreign robbers" were responsible. When Sophocles makes his Chorus of Theban elders declare that "religion is dying" because of the apparent nonfulfilment of the oracles, we should allow them to mean what they say. This is the Chorus which indicated their religious despair by asking (and we used the question in order to distinguish Sophocles' piety from Aeschylus's): "Why should I take part in the sacred dance?" Theirs is the voice of Theban religious practice; they lend the present crisis a full and obvious urgency.

It is therefore an ultimately fortunate thing that the parricide and incest should be established, and that the construction of events now prevailing, the humanly more comfortable but religion-wasting construction, should be refuted. The outcome of the play is a dreadful necessity, paradoxically divine and also embracing Oedipus's individual fate since yet another oracle has pronounced, this time in answer to Oedipus himself, that (as he reports)

I must live in incest with my mother, and bring before my fellow men a family they will not bear to look upon, and kill the father who begat me.

By exposing the full horror of the situation Oedipus demonstrates that things have come out right; nature follows the divine plan, experience is sanctified. And the long search which achieves this is his own: we are defining the sense in which the role of Oedipus is heroic.

If these facts within the Sophoclean play have not received attention, it is largely because of the presupposition that dramatic action is bound to be crude and dull and mechanical when it is determined from above—in the present case by oracle and prophecy.

The outraged individual of Romantic criticism is again to the fore, in consideration of Oedipus's sins; not only did he proceed in ignorance that the old man whom he attacked (after extreme provocation) was his father, and that the woman whom he subsequently married was his mother, but he was fated to do these things. The question of acting in ignorance need not detain us, since for Sophocles in this play, as for Aeschylus, psychophysical defilement follows the deed without regard to intention. But the divine binding of Oedipus to his fate has a daunting and detailed rigidity which the inherited curse and prophecy seem never to impart in Aeschylus. It suggests the determined movement of the stars which is a leading image of Sophoclean mutability. And indeed the stage downfall of Oedipus is the acting out of that lyrically foreshadowed mutability—but only in part, since the circling Bear is used by Sophocles to present a single cyclical movement bringing sorrow to one and joy to another. Romantic concentration on the figure of the king blinds us to the plight of Thebes and its final remedy; the city's terrible sickness, which overshadows everything else at the beginning of the play, is the result of harbouring a defilement, and it is cured by that single process of self-discovery leading to expulsion from the city which we incline to think of solely as Oedipus's tragedy.

The final impression of accomplishment is at one with the doubleness characterising Sophoclean mutability; the Chorus's vision of Oedipus "with his life reversed"—the thematic strand which criticism has gathered up gratefully—issues from a corporate consciousness occupied with divine fulfilment and the city's health; and the play comes to rest in a conclusion adequate to their anxieties. We return to our earlier insistence that the relationship of prosperity and adversity within the mutability-rhythm is symphonic rather than antithetical, its application at this moment being that the image of Oedipus falling as Thebes rises must be judged insufficient—insufficient and also misleading in that a number of false conclusions flow from it. In particular, it is impossible to invoke the late-classical Wheel of Fortune (or anything like it) without reducing Oedipus's downfall, and the saving of Thebes together with her religion, to complete aesthetic penury: we then have a mechanical and determinist scheme of no interest, both on the universal plane of mutability—the Bear's course is fixed—and in the plot of *Oedipus the King* which simply follows the course laid down for it in Apollo's oracle.

That Sophocles is not at all like this is a mystery experienced at the outset in the bright lyrical freedom investing his images of mutability; and the fullest human reflection of this mystery, we have already observed, is the binding of Oedipus to his fate. One or two considerations are relevant. Oedipus's dramatic solitude—the solitude of the single-handed sustainer of the action—coexists with a high measure of social integration. His relation to the people of Thebes is quasi-paternal; he calls them "my children" in the first words of the play; he insists that he is carrying the sorrows of the whole city on his shoulders. And it follows that our symphonic apprehension of opposite fortunes must be pursued within his single destiny: the sense in which his downfall means his city's salvation is immediate and intimate. It is true that Oedipus does not console himself, when disaster strikes him down, with the thought that his ruin is inextricably bound up with his city's deliverance from the killing plague. But the genius of this play is not compensatory. In any case, the spectator's point of view is not his. And when we do examine his own attitude, something of interest emerges.

Oedipus surveys his sins in two different ways. On the one hand he laments the pollution into which he has blundered. He has a lot to say about his ignorance of the true circumstances, but his motive in this is not to deny or even to mitigate culpability. He is exposing a might-have-been (or rather, a would-not-have-been: the analogy suggests itself of Antigone declaring the circumstances in which she would have left a relative unburied); he is saying that he would not have killed Laius or married Jocasta if he had known who they were. This situation-rooted simplicity is fundamental, it must not be perverted into false moral sophistication.

On the other hand Oedipus has an attitude to his sins which is narrowly institutional. Early in the play, when he is setting out to solve the mystery of Laius's death, he pronounces a solemn religious curse upon the unknown murderer, and this curse is treated as a fixed point of religio-moral reference as the story unfolds. Therefore *Oedipus the King* accommodates the formal curse on the sinner alongside the fact of his sin. The seer Teiresias, who is the first to state the truth, proceeds by way of directly accusing Oedipus of the polluting deeds, and at the same time charges him to "abide by the decree of your own mouth." Later, when it begins to dawn on Oedipus himself that the old man whom he killed long ago was none other than Laius, he cries out: "Unhappy me! It seems I have just been placing myself under a dreadful curse—and never knew." And later again:

> Suppose this stranger had any blood-connection with Laius—then who is now more miserable than the man before you, who more loathed of heaven? Neither stranger nor citizen is allowed to receive him; no one may speak to him; all must repel him from their homes. And it was my mouth and nobody else's that laid this—this curse—upon me.

He also refers his final expulsion, when it occurs, to this initial curse (which was coupled with a command to the people of Thebes not to shelter or have social or religious communication with the murderer): "noblest of Thebans, I have doomed myself to banishment by my command that all should thrust out the man of sin"; and a messenger describes how Oedipus shouted out for somebody to unbar the palace gates, "purposing to expel himself from the land—at once, so as not to bring the house under his own curse."

Thus a double representation of Oedipus's sins persists throughout; the curse and the discovered acts of pollution are two ways of stating the single fact of his guilt, and so far from the curse being absorbed within the parricide and incest (when these are established), it continues to the end, undiminished. It is plain from Oedipus's manner of shifting between "I was fated" and "I have doomed myself" that he regards both representations as adequate to his case, and we should surely be mistaken in supposing that he manipulates them advisedly. They are nothing more than modes of statement lying at hand, probably not even conceived as alternatives. The importance for us of this double representation resides in the sins themselves; the whole colour of unwitting guilt is changed when we observe the guilty sufferer apprehending himself as heaven's victim and, at the same time and indifferently, as self-doomed. The individual is no longer simply set upon from above, and a crude unilinear determinism gives place to something not entirely unlike the complex of human freedom and divine omnipotence in ordinary Christian belief—something that mystifies the observer from afar, an apparently pointless binocular agility.

Further, Oedipus's representation "I have doomed myself" does not indicate his surrender to a kind of trick, as though he had set a trap and then fallen into it himself; for the curse is a trap (if we are to save this analogy) in which only the guilty man can be caught. Moreover, it is a trap created and maintained by an expressive act of self-realisation within the play—by the king's utterance of a formal religious curse, and for this reason the language of self-doom cannot be pressed too literally. Our tendency to be repelled by what seems mechanical and unfeeling is due in part to a falsely limited understanding of the ritual act's externality; underestimating the principle of the self's presence in the "mere" deed, we resent the spectacle of his self-uttered doom bearing down on the human agent senselessly, inhumanly, from behind and beyond him.

These are points of substance for the entire unitary action of *Oedipus the King,* as well as for Oedipus's conception of his guilt; given due prominence they modify our experience of discontinuity between the world of human affairs and the dense tissue of oracle and prophecy controlling (but not only controlling) that world. And so the corporate consciousness surprises us, as Oedipus's does, by its enfolding within acknowledgment of responsibility the alien, the superhuman and the uncontrollable. When Oedipus warns Teiresias to mind his words since he is too weak to save himself from punishment, the seer twice answers that he is strong in the truth which he holds; he indicates what has already been noted—that prophecy is present possession of the invincible truth, and he invites its general application to Thebes and her troubles: disclosure of what lies ahead is secondary to exposure of what lies within, and contemplation of what lies within evokes in the diseased community, as in its king, the double response to a helpless victim and of one who is blameworthy. The Chorus carry the play's omnipresent doubleness upon a corporate voice of timorous, oscillatory conjecture.

In this manner, as it seems to me, the single distinct action in which Oedipus lays bare his own sins and discovers who he is escapes from critical entanglement with a false humanity, and floats free into a Sophoclean independence and self-poise. Humanity is not banished; it colours the action in precisely the fashion of the great central irony of Oedipus's ignorance of what he is doing: this fulfils the apparently artless function (in relation to the automatic guilt of pollution) of keeping alive awareness of a situational might-have-been; of suffusing the parricide and incest in solemn religious contemplation of that mere absence of knowledge in the human individual but for which these horrors would never have been perpetrated. Ironical this surely is, and altogether Sophoclean; and to Sophoclean irony we must join the even more popular subject of *hubris.* "I will start afresh," says Oedipus at the beginning of his search, "and once again bring dark things to the light." How are we to take this reference to his solution of the Sphinx's riddle, and this promise to repeat his success? The usual procedure (vaguely devised and executed) has been to assemble his two or three assertions of this kind and to inflate them, along with his remarks about the fallibility of human prophecy, into a hubristic correlative of the ruin that overtakes him. But this is patently unacceptable—not because the fault is incommensurate with the punishment, but because it bears no relation to the actions from which guilt and suffering flow. It is futile to think in terms of a peremptory, self-confident autocrat who stumbles in his pride, when Sophocles takes pains to show us that Oedipus received Apollo's oracle with pious seriousness and left his home and family in an attempt to escape its fulfilment; the intelligible connection which we observe, for example, between Macbeth's half-stifled ambition and his crimes and tormented conscience, is simply not to be found, nor anything like it.

That this entire method is misconceived becomes plain from a moment's consideration of the underlying necessity that the god's word shall prevail. Then why (it may be asked) does Sophocles bother to create Oedipus peremptory and self-confident? The broad Aristotelian answer is the correct one: a multicoloured portrait is more interesting than a portrait in monochrome. In other words, a hubristic colouring of Oedipus's search for the murderer is what Sophocles is aiming at; the moral import of his proud confidence is carried in the *laying bare* of his sins; it is not supposed to throw light on, or be in some way adequate to, the sins themselves. In this respect we must approach the play with modest expectations. Oedipus's solution of the Sphinx's riddle, that feat which is stressed throughout, has only the limited significance that it places him on a high eminence of achievement and reputation as a mystery-solver. He is in a position which Greek tragedy habitually surrounds in an atmosphere of religious dread, because it is very difficult, so the Greeks believed, to excel and still to avoid *hubris*.

Oedipus fails to avoid *hubris:* he is confident of his own success, he is quick to accuse Teiresias and Creon of plotting against his royal person and station, he remarks with near-contempt the fallibility of the god's human ministers (while retaining an entirely respectful attitude towards the god himself); and it is a sufficient indication of the gulf dividing Sophocles from ourselves that the hubristic taint to Oedipus's search affords the dramatist and his audience a satisfying commentary on the action. A second and almost equally alien function of Oedipus's lonely eminence is to initiate the double reversal in which he and Teiresias, and he and Creon, are involved. Oedipus first appears as a man of paranormal vision, able to discern that which is obscure to others; at the end, the teleological blindness of his common humanity has been declared through his blundering against the hard and hidden truth, and is paralleled in his self-inflicted physical blindness. Teiresias is introduced in the helplessness of blind old age; he is taunted by Oedipus for his want of eyes; he utters the prophecy that Oedipus shall end his days "a blind man, who now has sight." Oedipus cries out when he begins to suspect the truth: "I dread the seer can see," and it is part of the final vindication of the divine order that all are brought to realise that Teiresias can see indeed.

Hence the double reversal in which Oedipus moves from sight to blindness and Teiresias from blindness to sight. The relationship between these two individuals elaborates the primary double reversal in the fortunes of the city and its king. So does that between Oedipus and Creon. After Oedipus has publicly accused him of treachery, Creon declares: "It is not right to pronounce bad men good at random, or good men bad." His words point to the end of the play where, in the moment of full revelation, Oedipus discovers himself "most vile" (*kakistos*) and Creon, in immediate juxtaposition, "most noble" (*aristos*). The seeming traitor becomes the city's upright king (Creon succeeds Oedipus with an instant demonstration of just authority) while the king falls to the level of blind exiled beggar, the proven source of corporate pollution.

This festooning of quasi-mathematical symmetries is germane to dramatic intention and effect throughout *Oedipus the King,* working at the level of overall oppositions and transverse movements, and evident also in details of phrasing. We recognise Creon's "Don't judge bad men good or good men bad" for a characteristic Sophoclean turn, and one which we do not readily respond to; the utterance seems irrelevant in its first part (since Creon is here merely defending himself—saying that he is a good man who is being judged bad) and woodenly sententious in its entirety. But "Don't judge bad men good" has a hidden reference, which an audience familiar with the myth will have seized on, to Oedipus's as yet unexposed sins: the symmetry is fast maturing on the stage, and what strikes us as sententious and generalised will have gratified imaginations that were in love with structural proportion. So pervasive is this quasi-mathematical mode of Sophoclean Tragedy that it sometimes produces a paralysis of taste and intelligence in the professional classical scholar, so that in Jebb's very literate (if dated) translation of *Oedipus the King* we come across grotesque contortions like "a solitary man could not be held the same with that band" and "how can my sire be level with him who is as nought to me?." It is a pleasant irony that the scholars who are busy impressing on us the continuities of our cultural tradition should so clearly refute themselves in their instinctive vestigial honesty towards the strange texts they are rendering.

Like the quasilegal mode which occupied us earlier, over the *Antigone,* this endless contrasting and comparing (to which Aristotle extends a due dynamism in his concepts of Discovery and Reversal) springs from Tragedy's contact with fifth-century democratic institutions and with the fast developing art of prose. And again we must insist that the issue of this contact falls within the tragic idea; it is no mere accretion. We have invoked the language of symphonic mutability and of fearless outwardness in the conception and dramatic deployment of action, in order to suggest how this was so.

On Misunderstanding the *Oedipus Rex*

E. R. Dodds

On the last occasion when I had the misfortune to examine in Honour Moderations at Oxford I set a question on the *Oedipus Rex,* which was among the books prescribed for general reading. My question was "In what sense, if in any, does the *Oedipus Rex* attempt to justify the ways of God to man?" It was an optional question; there were plenty of alternatives. But the candidates evidently considered it a gift: nearly all of them attempted it. When I came to sort out the answers I found that they fell into three groups.

The first and biggest group held that the play justifies the gods by showing—or, as many of them said, "proving"—that we get what we deserve. The arguments of this group turned upon the character of Oedipus. Some considered that Oedipus was a bad man: look how he treated Creon—naturally the gods punished him. Others said "No, not altogether bad, even in some ways rather noble; but he had one of those fatal ἁμαρτίαι that all tragic heroes have, as we know from Aristotle. And since he had a ἁμαρτία he could of course expect no mercy: the gods had read the *Poetics.*" Well over half the candidates held views of this general type.

A second substantial group held that the *Oedipus Rex* is "a tragedy of destiny." What the play "proves," they said, is that man has no free will but is a puppet in the hands of the gods who pull the strings that make him dance. Whether Sophocles thought the gods justified in treating their puppet as they did was not always clear

From *Greece and Rome* 13, no. 1 (April 1966). © 1966 by Oxford University Press.

from their answers. Most of those who took this view evidently disliked the play; some of them were honest enough to say so.

The third group was much smaller, but included some of the more thoughtful candidates. In their opinion Sophocles was "a pure artist" and was therefore not interested in justifying the gods. He took the story of Oedipus as he found it, and used it to make an exciting play. The gods are simply part of the machinery of the plot.

Ninety percent of the answers fell into one or the other of these three groups. The remaining ten percent had either failed to make up their minds or failed to express themselves intelligibly.

It was a shock to me to discover that all these young persons, supposedly trained in the study of classical literature, could read this great and moving play and so completely miss the point. For all the views I have just summarized are in fact demonstrably false (though some of them, and some ways of stating them, are more crudely and vulgarly false than others). It is true that each of them has been defended by some scholars in the past, but I had hoped that all of them were by now dead and buried. Wilamowitz thought he had killed the lot in an article published in *Hermes* (34 [1899]) more than half a century ago; and they have repeatedly been killed since. Yet their unquiet ghosts still haunt the examination-rooms of universities—and also, I would add, the pages of popular handbooks on the history of European drama. Surely that means that we have somehow failed in our duty as teachers?

It was this sense of failure which prompted me to attempt once more to clear up some of these ancient confusions. If the reader feels—as he very well may—that in this paper I am flogging a dead horse, I can only reply that on the evidence I have quoted the animal is unaccountably still alive.

I

I shall take Aristotle as my starting point, since he is claimed as the primary witness for the first of the views I have described. From the thirteenth chapter of the *Poetics* we learn that the best sort of tragic hero is a man highly esteemed and prosperous who falls into misfortune because of some serious (μεγάλη) ἁμαρτία: examples, Oedipus and Thyestes. In Aristotle's view, then, Oedipus's misfortune was directly occasioned by some serious ἁμαρτία; and since Aristotle was known to be infallible, Victorian critics proceeded at once to look for this ἁμαρτία. And so, it appears, do the majority of present-day undergraduates.

What do they find? It depends on what they expect to find. As we all know, the word ἁμαρτία is ambiguous: in ordinary usage it is sometimes applied to false moral judgments, sometimes to purely intellectual error—the average Greek did not make our sharp distinction between the two. Since *Poetics* 13 is in general concerned with the moral character of the tragic hero, many scholars have thought in the past (and many undergraduates still think) that the ἁμαρτία of Oedipus must in Aristotle's view be a moral fault. They have accordingly gone over the play with a microscope looking for moral faults in Oedipus, and have duly found them—for neither here nor anywhere else did Sophocles portray that insipid and unlikely character, the man of perfect virtue. Oedipus, they point out, is proud and overconfident; he harbors unjustified suspicions against Teiresias and Creon; in one place he goes so far as to express some uncertainty about the truth of oracles. One may doubt whether this adds up to what Aristotle would consider μεγάλη ἁμαρτία. But even if it did, it would have no direct relevance to the question at issue. Years before the action of the play begins, Oedipus was already an incestuous parricide; if that was a punishment for his unkind treatment of Creon, then the punishment preceded the crime—which is surely an odd kind of justice.

"Ah," says the traditionalist critic, "but Oedipus's behaviour on the stage reveals the man he always was: he was punished for his basically unsound character." In that case, however, someone on the stage ought to tell us so: Oedipus should repent, as Creon repents in the *Antigone;* or else another speaker should draw the moral. To ask about a character in fiction "Was he a good man?" is to ask a strictly meaningless question: since Oedipus never lived we can answer neither "Yes" nor "No." The legitimate question is "Did Sophocles intend us to think of Oedipus as a good man?" This *can* be answered—not by applying some ethical yardstick of our own, but by looking at what the characters in the play say about him. And by that test the answer is "Yes." In the eyes of the Priest in the opening scene he is the greatest and noblest of men, the saviour of Thebes who with divine aid rescued the city from the Sphinx. The Chorus has the same view of him: he has proved his wisdom, he is the darling of the city, and never will they believe ill of him (l. 504ff.). And when the catastrophe comes, no one turns round and remarks "Well, but it was your own fault: it must have been; Aristotle says so."

In my opinion, and in that of nearly all Aristotelian scholars since Bywater, Aristotle does *not* say so; it is only the perversity of moralizing critics that has misrepresented him as saying so. It is almost certain that Aristotle was using ἁμαρτία here as he uses ἁμάρτημα in the *Nicomachean Ethics* (1135^{b}12) and in the *Rhetoric* (1374^{b}6), to mean an offence committed in ignorance of some material fact and therefore free from πονηρία or κακία. These parallels seem decisive; and they are confirmed by Aristotle's second example—Thyestes, the man who ate the flesh of his own children in the belief that it was butcher's meat, and who subsequently begat a child on his own daughter, not knowing who she was. His story has clearly much in common with that of Oedipus, and Plato as well as Aristotle couples the two names as examples of the gravest ἁμαρτία (*Laws* 838c). Thyestes and Oedipus are both of them men who violated the most sacred of Nature's laws and thus incurred the most horrible of all pollutions; but they both did so without πονηρία, for they knew not what they did—in Aristotle's quasi-legal terminology, it was a ἁμάρτημα, not an ἀδίκημα. That is why they were in his view especially suitable subjects for tragedy. Had they acted knowingly, they would have been inhuman monsters, and we could not have felt for them that pity which tragedy ought to produce. As it is, we feel both pity, for the fragile estate of man, and terror, for a world whose laws we do not understand. The ἁμαρτία of Oedipus did not lie in losing his temper with Teiresias; it lay quite simply in parricide and incest—a μεγάλη ἁμαρτία indeed, the greatest a man can commit.

The theory that the tragic hero must have a grave moral flaw, and its mistaken ascription to Aristotle, has had a long and disastrous history. It was gratifying to Victorian critics, since it appeared to fit certain plays of Shakespeare. But it goes back much further, to the seventeenth-century French critic Dacier, who influenced the practice of the French classical dramatists, especially Corneille, and was himself influenced by the still older nonsense about "poetic justice"—the notion that the poet has a moral duty to represent the world as a place where the good are always rewarded and the bad are always punished. I need not say that this puerile idea is completely foreign to Aristotle and to the practice of the Greek dramatists; I only mention it because on the evidence of those Honour Mods. papers it would appear that it still lingers on in some youthful minds like a cobweb in an unswept room.

To return to the *Oedipus Rex,* the moralist has still one last card to play. Could not Oedipus, he asks, have escaped his doom if he had been more careful? Knowing that he was in danger of committing parricide and incest, would not a really prudent man have avoided quarrelling, even in self-defence, with men older than himself, and also love-relations with women older than himself? Would he not, in Waldock's ironic phrase, have compiled a handlist of all the things he must not do? In real life I suppose he might. But we are not entitled to blame Oedipus either for carelessness in failing to compile a handlist or for lack of self-control in failing to obey its injunctions. For no such possibilities are mentioned in the play, or even hinted at; and it is an essential critical principle that *what is not mentioned in the play does not exist.* These considerations would be in place if we were examining the conduct of a real person. But we are not: we are examining the intentions of a dramatist, and we are not entitled to ask questions that the dramatist did not intend us to ask. There is only one branch of literature where we *are* entitled to ask such questions about τὰ ἐκτὸς τοῦ δράματος, namely the modern detective story. And despite certain similarities the *Oedipus Rex* is not a detective story but a dramatized folktale. If we insist on reading it as if it were a law report we must expect to miss the point.

In any case, Sophocles has provided a conclusive answer to those who suggest that Oedipus could, and therefore should, have avoided his fate. The oracle was *unconditional* (l. 790): it did not say "If you do so-and-so you will kill your father"; it simply said "You will kill your father, you will sleep with your mother." And what an oracle predicts is bound to happen. Oedipus does what he can to evade his destiny: he resolves never to see his supposed parents again. But it is quite certain from the first that his best efforts will be unavailing. Equally unconditional was the original oracle given to Laius (l. 711ff.): Apollo said that he *must* (χρῆναι) die at the hands of Jocasta's child; there is no saving clause. Here there is a significant difference between Sophocles and Aeschylus. Of Aeschylus's trilogy on the House of Laius only the last play, the *Septem,* survives. Little is known of the others, but we do know, from *Septem* 742ff., that according to Aeschylus the oracle given to Laius *was* conditional: "Do not beget a child; for *if* you do, that child will kill you." In Aeschylus the disaster *could* have been avoided, but Laius sinfully disobeyed and his sin brought ruin to his descendants. In Aeschylus the story was, like the *Oresteia,* a tale of crime and punishment; but Sophocles chose otherwise—that is why he altered the form of the oracle. There is no suggestion in the *Oedipus Rex* that Laius sinned or that Oedipus was the victim of an hereditary curse, and the critic must not assume what the poet has abstained from suggesting. Nor should we leap to the conclusion that Sophocles left out the hereditary curse because he thought the doctrine immoral; apparently he did not think so, since he used it both in the *Antigone* (l. 583ff.) and in the *Oedipus at Colonus* (l. 964ff.). What his motive may have been for ignoring it in the *Oedipus Rex* we shall see in a moment.

I hope I have now disposed of the moralizing interpretation, which has been rightly abandoned by the great majority of contemporary scholars. To mention only recent works in English, the books of Whitman, Waldock, Letters, Ehrenberg, Knox, and Kirkwood, however much they differ on other points, all agree about the essential moral innocence of Oedipus.

II

But what is the alternative? If Oedipus is the innocent victim of a doom which he cannot avoid, does this not reduce him to a mere puppet? Is not the whole play a "tragedy of destiny" which denies human freedom? This is the second of the heresies which I set out to refute. Many readers have fallen into it, Sigmund Freud among them (*The Interpretation of Dreams*); and you can find it confidently asserted in various popular handbooks, some of which even extend the assertion to Greek tragedy in general—thus providing themselves with a convenient label for distinguishing Greek from "Christian" tragedy. But the whole notion is in fact anachronistic. The modern reader slips into it easily because *we* think of two clear-cut alternative views—either we believe in free will or else we are determinists. But fifth-century Greeks did not think in these terms any more than Homer did: the debate about determinism is a creation of Hellenistic thought. Homeric heroes have their predetermined "portion of life" (μοῖρα); they must die on their "appointed day" (αἴσιμον ἦμαρ); but it never occurs to the poet or his audience that this prevents them from being free agents. Nor did Sophocles intend that it should occur to readers of the *Oedipus Rex*. Neither in Homer nor in Sophocles does divine foreknowledge of certain events imply that all human actions are predetermined. If explicit confirmation of this is required, we have only to turn to lines 1230ff., where the Messenger emphatically distinguishes Oedipus's self-blinding as "voluntary" and "self-chosen" from the "involuntary" parricide and incest. Certain of Oedipus's past actions were fate-bound; but everything that he does on the stage from first to last he does as a free agent.

Even in calling the parricide and the incest "fate-bound" I have perhaps implied more than the average Athenian of Sophocles' day would have recognized. As A. W. Gomme put it, "the gods know the future, but they do not order it: they know who will win the next Scotland and England football match, but that does not alter the fact that the victory will depend on the skill, the determination, the fitness of the players, and a little on luck" (*More Essays in Greek History and Literature*). That may not satisfy the analytical philosopher, but it seems to have satisfied the ordinary man at all periods. Bernard Knox aptly quotes the prophecy of Jesus to St. Peter, "Before the cock crow, thou shalt deny me thrice." The Evangelists clearly did not intend to imply that Peter's subsequent action was "fate-bound" in the sense that he could not have chosen otherwise; Peter fulfilled the prediction, but he did so by an act of free choice.

In any case I cannot understand Sir Maurice Bowra's idea that the gods *force* on Oedipus the knowledge of what he has done. They do nothing of the kind; on the contrary, what fascinates us is the spectacle of a man freely choosing, from the highest motives, a series of actions which lead to his own ruin. Oedipus might have left the plague to take its course; but pity for the sufferings of his people compelled him to consult Delphi. When Apollo's word came back, he might still have left the murder of Laius uninvestigated; but piety and justice required him to act. He need not have forced the truth from the reluctant Theban herdsman; but because he cannot rest content with a lie, he must tear away the last veil from the illusion in which he has lived so long. Teiresias, Jocasta, the herdsman, each in turn tries to stop him, but in vain: he must read the last riddle, the riddle of his own life. The immediate cause of Oedipus's ruin is not "Fate" or "the gods"—no oracle said that he must discover the truth—and still less does it lie in his own weakness; what causes his ruin is his own strength and courage, his loyalty to Thebes, and his loyalty to the truth. In all this we are to see him as a free agent: hence the suppression of the hereditary curse. And his self-mutilation and self-banishment are equally free acts of choice.

Why does Oedipus blind himself? He tells us the reason (l. 1369 ff.): he has done it in order to cut himself off from all contact with humanity; if he could choke the channels of his other senses he would do so. Suicide would not serve his purpose: in the next world he would have to meet his dead parents. Oedipus mutilates himself because he can face neither the living nor the dead. But why, if he is morally innocent? Once again, we must look at the play through Greek eyes. The doctrine that nothing matters except the agent's intention is a peculiarity of Christian and especially of post-Kantian thought. It is true that the Athenian law courts took account of intention: they distinguished as ours do between murder and accidental homicide or homicide committed in the course of self-defence. If Oedipus had been tried before an Athenian court he would have been acquitted—of murdering his father. But no human court could acquit him of pollution; for pollution inhered in the act itself, irrespective of motive. Of that burden Thebes could not acquit Oedipus, and least of all could its bearer acquit himself.

The nearest parallel to the situation of Oedipus is in the tale which Herodotus tells about Adrastus, son of Gordies. Adrastus was the involuntary slayer of his own brother, and then of Atys, the son of his benefactor Croesus; the latter act, like the killing of Laius, fulfilled an oracle. Croesus forgave Adrastus because the killing was unintended (ἀέκων), and because the oracle showed that it was the will of "some god." But Adrastus did not forgive himself: he committed suicide, "conscious" says Herodotus, "that of all men known to him he bore the heaviest burden of disaster." It is for the same reason that Oedipus blinds himself. Morally innocent though he is and knows himself to be, the objective horror of his actions remains with him and he feels that he has no longer any place in human society. Is that simply archaic superstition? I think it is something more. Suppose a motorist runs down a man and kills him, I think he *ought* to feel that he has done a terrible thing, even if the accident is no fault of his: he has destroyed a human life, which nothing can restore. In the objective order it is acts that count, not intentions. A man who has violated that order may well feel a sense of guilt, however blameless his driving.

But my analogy is very imperfect, and even the case of Adrastus is not fully comparable. Oedipus is no ordinary homicide: he has committed the two crimes which above all others fill us with instinctive horror. Sophocles had not read Freud, but he knew how people *feel* about these things—better than some of his critics appear to do. And in the strongly patriarchal society of ancient Greece the revulsion would be even more intense than it is in our own. We have only read Plato's prescription for the treatment to be given to parricides (*Laws* 872cff.). For this deed, he says, there can be no purification: the parricide shall be killed, his body shall be laid naked at a crossroads outside the city, each officer of the State shall cast a stone upon it and curse it, and then the bloody remnant shall be flung outside the city's territory and left unburied. In all this he is probably following actual Greek practice. And if that is how Greek justice treated parricides, is it surprising that Oedipus treats himself as he does, when the great king, "the first of men," the man whose intuitive genius had saved Thebes, is suddenly revealed to himself as a thing so unclean that "neither the earth can receive it, nor the holy rain nor the sunshine endure its presence"?

III

At this point I am brought back to the original question I asked the undergraduates: does Sophocles in this play attempt to justify the ways of God to man? If "to justify" means "to explain in terms of *human* justice," the answer is surely "No." If human justice is the standard, then, as Waldock bluntly expressed it, "Nothing can excuse the gods, and Sophocles knew it perfectly well." Waldock does not, however, suggest that the poet intended any attack on the gods. He goes on to say that it is futile to look for any "message" or "meaning" in this play: "there is no meaning," he tells us, "in the *Oedipus Rex;* there is merely the terror of coincidence." Kirkwood seems to take a rather similar line: "Sophocles," he says, "has no theological pronouncements to make and no points of criticism to score." These opinions come rather close to, if they do not actually involve, the view adopted by my third and last group of undergraduates—the view that the gods are merely agents in a traditional story which Sophocles, a "pure artist," exploits for dramatic purposes without raising the religious issue or drawing any moral whatever.

This account seems to me insufficient; but I have more sympathy with it than I have with either of the other heresies. It reflects a healthy reaction against the old moralizing school of critics; and the text of the play appears at first sight to support it. It is a striking fact that after the catastrophe no one on the stage says a word either in justification of the gods or in criticism of them. Oedipus says "These things were Apollo"—and that is all. If the poet has charged him with a "message" about divine justice or injustice, he fails to deliver it. And I fully agree that there is no reason at all why we should require a dramatist—even a Greek dramatist—to be for ever running about delivering banal "messages." It is true that when a Greek dramatic poet had something he passionately wanted to say to his fellow citizens he felt entitled to say it. Aeschylus in the *Oresteia*, Aristophanes in the *Frogs,* had something to say to their people and used the opportunity of saying it on the stage. But these are exceptional cases—both these works were produced at a time of grave crisis in public affairs—and even here the "message" appears to me to be incidental to the true function of the artist, which I should be disposed to define, with Dr. Johnson, as "the enlargement of our sensibility." It is unwise to generalize from special cases. (And, incidentally, I wish undergraduates would stop writing essays which begin with the words "This play *proves* that. . . ." Surely no work of art can ever "prove" anything: what value could there be in a "proof" whose premisses are manufactured by the artist?)

Nevertheless, I cannot accept the view that the *Oedipus Rex* conveys *no* intelligible meaning and that Sophocles' plays tell us nothing of his opinions concerning the gods. Certainly it is always dangerous to use dramatic works as evidence of their author's opinions, and especially of their religious convictions: we can legitimately discuss religion *in* Shakespeare, but do we know anything at all about the religion *of* Shakespeare? Still, I think I should venture to assert two things about Sophocles' opinions:

First, he did not believe (or did not always believe) that the gods are in any human sense "just";

Secondly, he did not always believe that the gods exist and that man should revere them.

The first of these propositions is supported not only by the implicit evidence of the *Oedipus Rex* but by the explicit evidence of another play which is generally thought to be close in date to it. The closing lines of the *Trachiniae* contain a denunciation in violent terms of divine injustice. No one answers it. I can only suppose that the poet had no answer to give.

For the second of my two propositions we have quite strong *external* evidence—which is important, since it is independent of our subjective impressions. We know that Sophocles held various priesthoods; that when the cult of Asclepius was introduced to Athens he acted as the god's host and wrote a hymn in his honour; and that he was himself worshipped as a "hero" after his death, which seems to imply that he accepted the religion of the State and was accepted by it. But the external evidence does not stand alone: it is strongly supported by at least one passage in the *Oedipus Rex*. The celebrated choral ode about the decline of prophecy and the threat to religion was of course suggested by the scene with Creon which precedes it; but it contains generalizations which have little apparent relevance either to Oedipus or to Creon. Is the piety of this ode purely conventional, as Whitman maintained in a vigorous but sometimes perverse book? One phrase in particular seems to forbid this interpretation. If men are to lose all respect for the gods, in that case, the Chorus asks, τί δεῖ με χορεύειν; (l. 895). If by this they mean merely "Why should I, a Theban elder, dance?", the question is irrelevant and even slightly ludicrous; the meaning is surely "Why should I, an Athenian citizen, continue to serve in a chorus?" In speaking of themselves as a chorus they step out of the play into the contemporary world, as Aristophanes' choruses do in the *parabasis*. And in effect the question they are asking seems to be this: "If Athens loses faith in religion, if the views of the Enlightenment prevail, what significance is there in tragic drama, which exists as part of the service of the gods?" To that question the rapid decay of tragedy in the fourth century may be said to have provided an answer.

In saying this, I am not suggesting with Ehrenberg that the character of Oedipus reflects that of Pericles, or with Knox that he is intended to be a symbol of Athens: allegory of that sort seems to me wholly alien to Greek tragedy. I am only claiming that at one point in this play Sophocles took occasion to say to his fellow citizens something which he felt to be important. And it *was* important, particularly in the period of the Archidamian War, to which the *Oedipus Rex* probably belongs. Delphi was known to be pro-Spartan: that is why Euripides was given a free hand to criticize Apollo. But if Delphi could not be trusted, the whole fabric of traditional belief was threatened with collapse. In our society religious faith is no longer tied up with belief in prophecy; but for the ancient world, both pagan and Christian, it was. And in the years of the Archidamian War belief in prophecy was at a low ebb; Thucydides is our witness to that.

I take it, then, as reasonably certain that while Sophocles did not pretend that the gods are in any human sense just he nevertheless held that they are entitled to our worship. Are these two opinions incompatible? Here once more we cannot hope to understand Greek literature if we persist in looking at it through Christian spectacles. To the Christian it is a necessary part of piety to believe that God is just. And so it was to Plato and to the Stoics. But the older world saw no such necessity. If you doubt this, take down the *Iliad* and read Achilles' opinion of what divine justice amounts to (24.525–33); or take down the Bible and read the Book of Job. Disbelief in divine justice as measured by human yardsticks can perfectly well be associated with deep religious feeling. "Men," said Heraclitus, "find some things unjust, other things just; but in the eyes of God all things are beautiful and good and just." I think that Sophocles would have agreed. For him, as for Heraclitus, there is an objective world order which man must respect, but which he cannot hope fully to understand.

IV

Some readers of the *Oedipus Rex* have told me that they find its atmosphere stifling and oppressive: they miss the tragic exaltation that one gets from the *Antigone* or the *Prometheus Vinctus*. And I fear that what I have said here has done nothing to remove that feeling. Yet it is not a feeling which I share myself. Certainly the *Oedipus Rex* is a play about the blindness of man and the desperate insecurity of the human condition: in a sense every man must grope in the dark as Oedipus gropes, not knowing who he is or what he has to suffer; we all live in a world of appearance which hides from us who-knows-what dreadful reality. But surely the *Oedipus Rex* is also a play about human greatness. Oedipus is great, not in virtue of a great worldly position—for his worldly position is an illusion which will vanish like a dream—but in virtue of his inner strength: strength to pursue the truth at whatever personal cost, and strength to accept and endure it when found. "This horror is mine," he cries, "and none but I is *strong* enough to bear it." Oedipus is great because he accepts the responsibility for *all* his acts, including those which are objectively most horrible, though subjectively innocent.

To me personally Oedipus is a kind of symbol of the human intelligence which cannot rest until it has solved all the riddles—even the last riddle, to which the answer is that human happiness is built on an illusion. I do not know how far Sophocles intended that. But certainly in the last lines of the play (which I firmly believe to be genuine) he does generalize the case, does appear to suggest that in some sense Oedipus is every man and every man is potentially Oedipus. Freud felt this (he was not insensitive to poetry), but as we all know he understood it in a specific psychological sense. "Oedipus's fate," he says, "moves us only because it might have been our own, because the oracle laid upon us before birth the very curse which rested upon him. It may be that we were all destined to direct our first sexual impulses towards our mothers, and our first impulses of hatred and violence towards our fathers; our dreams convince us that we were." Perhaps they do, but Freud did not ascribe his interpretation of the myth to Sophocles, and it is not the interpretation I have in mind. Is there not in the poet's view a much wider sense in which every man is Oedipus? If every man could tear away the last veils of illusion, if he could see human life as time and the gods see it, would he not see that against that tremendous background all the generations of men are as if they had not been, ἴσα καὶ τὸ μηδὲν ξώσας? That was how Odysseus saw it when he had conversed with Athena, the embodiment of divine wisdom. "In Ajax' condition," he says, "I recognize my own: I perceive that all men living are but appearance or unsubstantial shadow."

> ὁρῶ γὰρ ἡμᾶς οὐδὲν ὄντας ἄλλο πλὴν
> εἴδωλ᾽, ὅσοιπερ ξῶμεν, ἢ κούφην σκιάν.

So far as I can judge, on this matter Sophocles' deepest feelings did not change. The same view of the human condition which is made explicit in his earliest extant play is implicit not only in the *Oedipus Rex* but in the *Oedipus Coloneus,* in the great speech where Oedipus draws the bitter conclusion from his life's experience and in the famous ode on old age. Whether this vision of man's estate is true or false I do not know, but it ought to be comprehensible to a generation which relishes the plays of Samuel Beckett. I do not wish to describe it as a "message." But I find in it an enlargement of sensibility. And that is all I ask of any dramatist.

The Innocence of Oedipus:
The Philosophers on *Oedipus the King*

Thomas Gould

E. R. Dodds has complained recently that the undergraduates at Oxford still read *Oedipus the King*, and Greek tragedy in general, in ignorance of the new enlightened thinking that they could have found in almost any scholarly work on the subject today ("On Misunderstanding the *Oedipus Rex*"). They drearily repeat, he says, the very misconceptions that Wilamowitz thought he had put an end to seventy years ago. He finds the idea still depressingly common, for instance, that Greek tragedies always show men coming to bad ends because of "tragic flaws" in their character. The students could have been disabused of this notion, Dodds points out, by reading any one of quite a number of excellent books or articles. Two of Dodds's complaints may not be as justified as this one, however. On two important counts the undergraduates seem to have been right and their examiner wrong. And since Dodds, quite correctly, implies that his views represent those of the majority among recent scholars, it is worth looking at these two points.

First, there is the general agreement among modern critics that the greatest of the Greek tragedies were never tragedies of fate, that, whatever the reader thinks who comes fresh to the text without the benefit of scholarly and critical works, the finest tragedies never show good men being crushed by destinies that they could not have avoided. To believe in tragedies of fate, according to Dodds and to many others, is worse even than to believe in a "tragic flaw."

The second point concerns Aristotle on the "tragic flaw." Did

From *Arion* 5, no. 4 (April 1966). © 1966 by the Trustees of Boston University.

he or did he not assert that in a play in which the protagonist is shown coming to grief the catastrophe must be felt to be due, at least in part, to some avoidable error on the part of the protagonist? Since Bywater's time, as Dodds says, more and more scholars have come to the conclusion that Aristotle required only that there be an unavoidable mistake in the facts. This is now the orthodox position. Yet ordinary readers, ignorant of the works of these critics, still tend to assume that Aristotle demanded a flaw in the protagonist's character or intellect.

I would like to champion the judgment of the naive reader on both of these questions.

There is a line of reasoning that goes something like this. If the *Oedipus* is a tragedy of fate, the story of a man who is ruined by forces he cannot be expected to have understood or influenced, then the protagonist of the story was obviously not responsible for his misery in any way. But if he was not responsible for what happened to him, he is a mere puppet and his story is sad, but not "tragic"; it cannot engage our moral sensibility and it cannot, therefore, be profound or moving. But the *Oedipus* is profound and moving. Therefore it is not a tragedy of fate.

If we ask someone who feels this way about the play just why he wants Oedipus to be "responsible," we usually get a rather complicated answer. First of all it will be vigorously denied, more than likely, that what is wanted is that our playwrights show us punishments fitting crimes—a world where the good are always rewarded and the bad made to pay for their failings. If we admitted this we would be admitting that Aristotle's theory of the "tragic flaw" (interpreted in the old-fashioned way) was really right after all. Whatever is meant by "responsible" in this context, it is usually not the same as criminal guilt. What is wanted, apparently, is "free will" or "free choice" in the protagonist's actions. "What fascinates us," Dodds suggests, "is the spectacle of a man freely choosing from the highest motives a series of actions which lead to his own ruin." Oedipus must be innocent of harboring any culpable desires, then; and yet it must be he, acting freely, who brought on the catastrophe, not the gods, not fate.

There is a muddle here somewhere, surely. Oedipus's intentions were good, but the results of his actions were bad; and the explanation for this is that he did not have certain important pieces of information. One would have thought that we were reduced to one of two possibilities. Either Oedipus could not have come into possession of the important facts however much he had improved his intelligence or character, which would mean that something else must have been at fault for his catastrophe—chance, the world, fate, or the gods. Or Oedipus brought his misery upon himself and nothing external is to be blamed, in which case it must be true that Oedipus would have been able to avoid his catastrophe had he been a better man or at least a better thinker. Yet, according to the theory we are considering, neither of these is the case: it is denied that Oedipus is brought down by things external to him, but it is also denied that his uncompelled moves were bad or foolish in any way.

There are two favorite ways of coping with this difficulty. Sometimes it is suggested that Oedipus would not have avoided his misery by having been a better man, but he *could* have remained prosperous and happy if he had been a *less* good man. I shall examine this strange theory. . . below. The other way out is to point to the fact that the Greeks before the Stoics had not yet conceived of the will as we do and so did not see fate and free will as exclusive alternatives. That is, if we think away "our" notion of the will and accept Sophocles' idea of it, we will be able to see that Oedipus acted freely and was responsible for what happened even though the whole sequence of events is repeatedly said to be the work of the gods.

Our first task, then, is to examine the difference between the ancient and the modern notions of the will.

Neither the poets nor the philosophers of classical Greece had any difficulty in distinguishing between voluntary and involuntary actions; between situations where a man could act as he saw fit and situations where, because of nature, the gods or other men, a man could not so act; between human acts in which the character of the actor could be read (and praised or blamed accordingly) and acts where nothing could be justly inferred about the character of the men involved, and so on. They also knew full well, of course, that some men were decisive, energetic and able to make their characters felt by the world, whereas others either lacked energy or opportunity or for some other reason did not so often or so effectively impress their unique personalities on the events in which they were involved. What, then, is meant by the complaint that the ancients did not have "our" notion of the will? Usually what is meant is that it rarely, if ever, occurred to the Greeks (before the Stoics and Epicureans) that in the act of making a decision a man is introducing a surge of energy (or a twist, or a focus) that could not be accounted for by the sum total of all antecedent events. The ancients tended to think that the crucial distinction was that between a man who is allowed to act according to his character and a man who is given no such opportunity; but they also thought that the character was probably determined by all of the things that had happened in his past (his habits, education, reading, accidental encounters, even the experiences in his previous lives, according to Plato, and certainly the experiences of his society even in the years before he was born). Modern readers, on the other hand, are very often made uncomfortable by this formulation. Unless the will can break the chains of efficient causes which are governed by unalterable mechanical laws, it is argued, we are not "free," and we cannot blame anyone for anything: a man's character would be made for him, not by him, and his every act would already be determined before he was born. In such an idea, it is feared, we have an intellectualized version of fatalism.

From Homer to Aristotle both poets and philosophers tended to ask not "was he free?" as we might do, but "is he responsible (aitios)?" The questions are the same in that they both are attempts to identify the extent to which events were in our power (ἐφ' ἡμῖν), so that we will be able to assign praise and blame with justice. They are different questions, however, in that the latter, the ancient question, is answered in the affirmative if it can be shown that the men involved acted according to their characters (ἦθος); the modern question, on the other hand, can on occasion be a request for something else in addition to this. It can also express a desire to know whether there were men involved in the events in question to whose inner tendencies or thoughts we can trace at least some of the real causes of the events—"causes" now being used, not in a practical sense (was he brought up well? should he be re-educated? must we try to change his character by persuasion or punishment?), but in a metaphysical sense (were there new beginnings, ἀρχαὶ κινήσεως, at the moments of decision-making which cannot be restated as effects of antecedent events?).

The ambiguity in the English word "responsible" is the cause of many misunderstandings. There are at least three things that we could mean when we ask to what extent a man is "responsible" for what he did. The word can mean (1) that the man so described acted in accordance with his own character, saying nothing about what determined that character, (2) that in addition to being "responsible" in this way, the man's character might have been different had he developed different habits in his past, saying nothing about what things would have had to be different in order that he should develop different habits, or (3) that in addition to these two requirements, somehow, either at the moment we are concentrating on or in the past when his character was being formed, there was within him somewhere a new beginning, a turn or an impulse that cannot be entirely accounted for by antecedent events.

Although the Greek word *aitios* was capable of the same ambiguities (Aristotle, *Nicomachean Ethics*), in the period before the Stoics and Epicureans, as I have said, it *almost* always meant the first, or the first combined with the second; the third possibility did not seem vital or appropriate. This restriction may have been, not a weakness, however, but the strength of the Greek moralists. With this meaning of "responsibility" they were able to distinguish clearly enough between moral and immoral actions; between the man who put a high value on looking ahead, calculating, moving with due forethought, etc., and the man who saw no value in such planning; between the man who hated the desires within his own psyche that were capable of leading him to self-defeating goals (the man of conscience, the man who could feel guilt) and the man who was too willing to look for purely external sources for his failures, and so on. By having nothing to do with the third sense of "responsibility," they could then concentrate on the circumstances that were responsible for a man's character's being what it was, in hopes always of finding something that could be changed in order to improve men's characters in the future.

The main difficulty, as the earlier Greeks saw it, was not in the nature of the will, but the consequences of the power and the intentions of the gods. Were the gods humane? all of them or merely some? could you choose your own divinity or did it choose you? was divinity all-powerful or not? did it care whether human beings were happy? were the rules that the gods themselves were subject to comforting or appalling things? One's tests for human "responsibility" necessarily varied according to the way one answered questions like these. And yet, because they *also* asked about the character of the man and whether or not he was acting gladly, the Greeks of the classical period stayed remarkably clear of the maze of puzzles that such questions could lead to; and they usually stayed clear of the

worst features of oriental fatalism also, even when their answers to
these questions about the gods were most bitter and pessimistic.

The *Iliad* already shows us a whole range of subtly different
attitudes toward the presence of the power of divinity. Paris was
thought by Hector and others to have drawn annoyingly incorrect
conclusions from the fact that human destinies are in the laps of the
gods. Once, when he is scolded by Helen, he tells her to stop crit-
icizing him: Menelaus had won this time, with the help of his god;
he, Paris, would win on some other occasions with the help of *his*
god (3.438ff., again at 6.339). But Hector had an even more appalling vision of the power of the gods or fate and of the helplessness of
men than Paris had (and Homer makes us feel that Hector was not
only perceptive but pious, too, and knew what he was talking about),
yet his fatalism did not tend to make him craven or self-indulgent at
all. Indeed, it made his criticism of his brother all the sharper. In one
breath Hector says that Zeus obviously sent Paris to be a bane to his
countrymen; in the next he wishes Paris would die swiftly; then he
goes off to see him in order to upbraid him and to change his ways
(6.280–5). Helen constantly criticizes *herself,* although she believes,
or says she believes, that the gods willed her disastrous yielding to
Paris (6.349; at 6.357–8 Helen makes a conjecture as to what the
purpose of the gods might have been). Helen struggles against her
daimōn, in marked contrast to Paris, who, when he is favored by the
same goddess, yields willingly and takes pride in the fact (3.65).
Although Helen blames herself—or rather *because* she blames herself—neither Hector nor Priam do blame her. I do not hold you
responsible (*aitiē*), says Priam. The gods are responsible in my eyes:

οὔ τί μοι αἰτίη ἐσσί· θεοί νύ μοι αἴτιοί εἰσιν.
(3.164ff.)

The elders agree, though they wish she would go away nevertheless.

In the fifth century Gorgias composed a defense of Helen in
which everything *but* character is given as a cause. The results are
startling. She could not be blamed, he says, because she must have
gone with Paris for one of four reasons (*aitiai*): either (1) because of
the plans of fortune (τυχῆς βουλήμασι) and the premeditations of
the gods, or (2) because she was seized by force, or (3) because she
was won over by reason, or (4) because she was captured by desire.
Euripides gives Helen a similar, though even more elaborate, defense
in the *Trojan Women;* but he then has Hecuba refute these reasons

(here called λόγοι) one by one. Hecuba's main weapon is to translate Helen's observations back into terms of the personal character implied. Thus Helen says that Aphrodite could not be resisted by a mortal; Hecuba retorts that "Aphrodite" is a misleading name for a certain well-known kind of weakness (ll. 988–99).

As Aeschylus tells the story, both Clytemnestra and Orestes committed crimes because the curse of the house of Atreus had to be worked out. Yet Aeschylus obviously disapproves of Clytemnestra, even though he portrays Orestes as entirely blameless. Clytemnestra can apparently be held responsible, despite the existence of the divine plan, because she was, nevertheless, acting willingly, according to her character—she saw the course of action open to her as one that fitted well with her vision of how she would like things to be. (Aegisthus was attractive and it was convenient that Agamemnon should be got out of the way.) The case was otherwise with Orestes: he was truly horrified by the demands of heaven. Apollo had repeatedly to impress on the young man that the consequences of not killing his mother would be even more revolting than the polluting crime itself. And so Orestes is thought admirable, Clytemnestra not.

A belief in fate or the ultimate triumph of divine will does not always make judgments of human excellence impossible or nonsensical. There are different ways of judging men implied in different conceptions of the divine will. According to the Stoics, for instance, the wise man is the man who, as he does what the rulers of the universe will have him do, finds that it is exactly what he would have wanted to do anyhow. ("Ducunt volentem fata, nolentem trahunt" [The Fates lead the man who is willing and drag the one who is not.], attributed by Seneca to Cleanthes.) On this theory, it is Clytemnestra, not Orestes, who acted well—if we can accept the curse as the plan of Providence. The Stoics, of course, denied that divinities could have conflicting desires or that different divinities were triumphant at different moments in history. For them, therefore, the discovery that someone did gladly what divinity would have him do was a sufficient test of that person's moral excellence. Aeschylus assumed that divinity could want for a man what a man ought not to want for himself; the Stoics were certain that doing the god's will—living according to nature—is invariably the shortest path to happiness, also to a feeling of freedom and to true goodness. Neither the Stoics nor Aeschylus, then, allowed their belief in the inevitable triumph of divine plans to deprive them of a way to distinguish good men from bad men. Indeed, their different conceptions of divinity helped define their different schemes for praise and blame.

But perhaps it is wrong to speak of the need to distinguish better men from worse men as though this were a secondary consideration. It is obviously primary. A society that deprived itself of the means to influence the character and desires of its members just could not last very long. And the most important means that it has to effect changes of this sort is to make its disapproval felt by a wrongdoer or potential wrongdoer and so make that person hate the part of himself that harbors the destructive desire. If we let a man who has acted regrettably speak blandly of forces external to his character, when the circumstances are the same once more he is likely to make the same disastrous move all over again. This is why Hector and Helen cannot allow Paris to lessen his disgrace by pointing to the role of the gods in his defeat, and why the Achaean princes cannot change their feelings toward Agamemnon even if they half accept his conjecture that it must have been a god who took his wits away the day that he alienated Achilles. Paris and Agamemnon are judged "responsible" in the sense that they acted according to their character; regrettable events were traced to regrettable tendencies in these men, and these tendencies were thought to be capable of being improved by the instillation of shame or guilt. They saw no inconsistency between this attitude and a belief in powerful and frequent divine interventions.

On the other hand, this does not mean that Homer or the tragedians thought that men were *never* able to lessen their responsibility for a crime or disastrous act by pointing to the role of the gods. We accept Patroclus's plea that he was not disgraced because Apollo and Zeus were really his killers, not Hector. And we accept Orestes' plea that Apollo forced him to kill his mother. It is entirely possible, therefore, that Sophocles meant us to accept Oedipus's plea that the gods, not he himself, are responsible for his wretchedness. If Sophocles were a Platonist or a Stoic or a Christian, then we would be right to insist that divine action alone could not be responsible for Oedipus's misery; but Sophocles was none of these things. Sophocles seems to have honored the gods and thought them wonderful and believed them to be on the side of excellence and justice in the long run; but so did Homer and Aeschylus. He seems to have accepted, with Homer and Aeschylus, the possibility that the gods could ruin the lives of excellent and well-intentioned men.

Sophocles could believe, then, that Oedipus was undone by external things and that Oedipus was in no way responsible for his misery; and yet this would not make him a universal fatalist. Nor would it make his Oedipus a puppet without character or excellence. There is nothing to prevent us from seeing what kind of man the protagonist of the story is—complicated, unique, conscientious, impetuous, brilliant—even if his major goals are hideously frustrated in the end. Sophocles no doubt assumed that many, perhaps most, men, good and bad, were given frequent opportunities to act according to their characters. It is evidently only very special men, in his belief, who are systematically prevented by divinity from pursuing their own goals. This is a vision of things that may baffle us or disappoint us (even while we are moved by the play itself), but the baffling or disappointing part is not the notion of the will that is implied; it is the conception of divinity. At least there is no obvious way that we can think away "our" notion of will and accept an older notion and so make Oedipus responsible for his own miseries again. . . .

The ancients talked of the power to do what one wants (or what seems best, or what really is best) and responsibility (the justice with which one could infer from an act whether or not the man was good) more often than they spoke of freedom. Nevertheless, their notions could easily be translated into terms of freedom—and sometimes were, as in *Republic* 8 and 9. They too, just like ourselves, assumed that freedom was a very desirable thing. They could imagine a man as being free, however, even if it were assumed that the causes for his actions could ultimately be traced to things outside himself. A man is free, they thought, if at least one of the possibilities presented to him is among those he could imagine with pleasure. If none appeals to him, he is under constraint, not free. They might also insist, as the Socratics did for instance, that if freedom is really a good thing, then an additional factor must be present: the thing that the man imagines with pleasure must be *correctly* imagined, i.e., if he gets what he wishes he will not be disappointed. His character must be such that when given a chance to act according to it, according to his own vision of what is worth pursuing, he will move toward the highest possible happiness. After all, the most obvious reason for calling a man's habits or his notion of what is valuable bad or foolish is that we think he is pursuing self-destructive goals. And a self-destructive goal is one which will eventually result in the disappearance of his freedom; he will find himself blocked, disheartened, frustrated, or actually restricted by society.

It will be noticed that this conception of the problem leaves plenty of room for "free" actions even if it is assumed, as it usually was in antiquity, that chance, nature, the gods, and the society that educated us were among them the real causes of men's characters being what they were. It did not occur to them—nor should it have—that just because the causes for our behavior can always be traced to things outside us in this manner, therefore there is no point in trying to change society, influence politics, sharpen the criteria for assigning praise and blame, revolutionize education, please the gods, and so on. If A moves to interfere with B's pursuit of what he thinks valuable (by calling B bad or foolish, or educating him, or having him arrested, or whatever) the appropriate question to ask is not did A's desire to interfere come into being ultimately as the result of causes outside of A, but will the results of the interference be good or bad? for A and B both or only for A? etc. The "lazy argument," as the Stoics called it (ὁ ἀργὸς λόγος), the conclusion that, because a man's recovery from an illness must be determined by things already in existence, therefore he will recover whether he calls a doctor or not, is fallacious. (See also Gilbert Ryle, *Dilemmas* [Cambridge 1954] chap. 2, "It was to Be.") One of the most crucial of the causes determining his recovery is the existence (or future existence, depending on how far back we go) of a conviction in his head that a doctor's presence would be desirable.

There are several reasons why modern readers find distasteful or inadequate this idea that one ought not to look at the causes of a man's character to find out if he is acting "freely"—the idea that freedom means only the opportunity to act according to one's character (or the opportunity so to act if one's character is good, if we follow the Socratic line). One reason is that, like the Hellenistic and Christian philosophers, we have a habit of looking not for those points in a chain of causes that are of greatest practical importance, but for ultimate origins. The philosophers of the classical period avoided much confusion, however, because they thought of a man's character primarily in terms of the vision of what is valuable that motivates him. Socrates catalogued men according to the thing they cherished most: wine, honor, wisdom, etc. (φίλοινοι, φιλότιμοι, φιλόσοφοι, κτλ. *Republic* 5.475). If we cling to that as what we most want to know when we ask what a man's character is, then, when we entertain the possibility that an observer might, with certain knowledge of our character and our situation, predict infallibly what we will do, even during those moments when we feel most free, the thought will just no longer disturb us. The causes of our characters will be sought in a practical spirit: if our vision of life has led us to unrewarding things, we shall look for those factors in our past—our education, our reading, and the values cherished by our society, for instance—that might profitably be *changed*.

But for many people this is not the end of the problem either. The difficulty that some find with the classical notion of the will is that it seems to them to be empty of everything that they mean when they say that they want to be "free." According to Plato a man is free if and only if he is motivated by a set of values that will not lead him into a trap; the man who is best equipped for life, as Aristotle puts it, is the person for whom what appears to be most worth pursuing and what really is worth pursuing are one and the same (*Nicomachean Ethics* 3.4). To do what you think to be to your benefit is useless, Socrates points out (*Gorgias* 466ff.), unless you are right that it will benefit you. The highest freedom, therefore, will be achieved if you are absolutely certain about the true good. In one sense, then, you have no choice at all when you are really free. Only one course of action is open to the truly free man, the one that he *knows* will lead to happiness.

There are in fact two main difficulties with this formulation of complete freedom, both felt already by the ancients themselves. First, it seems to violate our need to feel that we are each unique. If perfection in the art of living must be bought at the price of pursuing only what divinity and all other men want us to pursue, we would prefer (in some moods, anyhow) to remain imperfect; we cherish the right to make our own mistakes. Plato points out (*Republic* 9.590d–e) that all societies, without exception, must hold their young in check. They do not let them do what appears to them to be to their good, and they only liberate them and call them adult and responsible when they think that the young will want just what their elders want them to want. They assume that the children would not have been free if they had been let go while they still had immature desires. And in fact, Plato says, the truth can only make a few men free; the rest are so ill-equipped to understand the important things even in their mature years that their nearest approach to true freedom will be to be made by the laws to do what they would have wanted to do had they been as perspicacious as what they would have wanted to do had they been as perspicacious as the framers of those laws. That the ancients were perfectly capable of being made uncomfortable by this thought is clear from Plato's vigorous parody of the Democratic Man. Not that there is a clear way out of Plato's conclusion, however. Even the most eloquent defenders of the freedom to make mistakes (e.g., John Stuart Mill and Isaiah Berlin) have had to build their arguments largely on practical considerations. The issue is still very much alive, in any case, and is part of the quarrel between Catholics and Protestants, and that between Socialists and Capitalists (the Communist Party and the Catholic Church finding themselves bedfellows not for the first time).

The second difficulty with the notion that complete freedom is equivalent to having a perfect character is more serious. It involves the existence, power and benevolence of divinity. God's will is my freedom, says Epictetus. If we can learn to value what divinity (or Nature or Reason) would want us to value, then we will be free in the sense that (1) everything we want will be in our power and (2) there will be nothing more rewarding that we could have been pursuing instead. And yet, if one believes, as the Fathers of the Church were bound to do, for instance, that divinity could do anything it wanted to do and what it wanted for all of us was that we achieve this most rewarding of all possible kinds of freedom, then a new difficulty arises. How are we going to account for God's refusal to make himself manifest in all his glory so that we *must* choose him, or at least to have arranged things so that we never failed to do things his way in the end, to our own supreme benefit? If freedom in the highest sense is certainty about what it would be best for us to devote ourselves to, and God could give us this certainty any time he wished, why has he so far refused to do so? The Christian answer, of course, is to say that this is *not* freedom in the highest sense; freedom in the highest sense is the ability to make decisions in *uncertainty*. This is the other side of the notion that the best freedom is freedom to make our own mistakes. To be unerringly disposed, whether by passion or by intellect, toward our true well-being, plus living in a favorable time and place, then, is thought to be less desirable than to be allowed to do what merely appears to be for our own good, even when we know full well that we might be making a disastrous error; to be set alternatives one of which is demonstrably better than the other is thought to be less valuable than to be set alternatives neither one of which can be shown without a doubt to be preferable to the other. And so valuable is this freedom, it is believed, that God gives it to us knowing that it will mean that most of us will in our ignorance "choose" damnation.

No wonder, then, that we quite often get a complicated and rather muddy answer when we ask a modern reader of the *Oedipus* just what he means when he insists that the protagonist must have been "free." Inappropriate ideas—some charged with great emotion—are likely to crowd into our heads and prevent us from getting straight what actually happens in the course of the play.

We must first think away the Stoic and Christian contributions to the debate about "freedom," and then try to recover the excitement and confusion of the quarrel that involved sophists, poets and philosophers in Sophocles' Athens.

In *Republic* 2.380a, Socrates quotes from a lost play by Aeschylus where it is said that "god plants criminal responsibility in men,"

θεὸς μὲν αἰτίαν φύει βροτοῖς,

whenever he wishes to destroy a family utterly. Socrates is horrified. Divinity is not responsible (*aitios*) for all things good and bad, "as the many think"; it is responsible only for a few things in men's lives, Socrates insists (379c). "For the good things nothing else should be held responsible (*aitiateon*), but for evils other things, *not* god, must be sought as the cause (*aitia*)." The gods ruled the universe, Socrates and Plato thought, to the extent that the men of the most excellent character could be guaranteed to win the best things life has to offer. But the existence—indeed, predominance (*Republic* 2.379c4–5; *Laws* 9.906a)—of self-destructive energy in the world and in human moves proves that divinity is not able to do what would be best of all, to free everyone by giving them only true desires. Freedom is possible only for the wise, according to Socrates, and for those of the foolish who are lucky enough to be trained and governed by the wise. Although the gods presumably want us all to be happy and can guarantee that all who are truly perceptive will be so, they cannot obliterate those features of incarnate existence that make men less than perfectly perceptive.

The philosophers were right when they insisted that the tragedians did not see things in this light. Sophocles represents the gods as invariably getting their way, although at the expense of the happiness of many a good man. He regularly shows the gods as operating on a scale of values that cuts across the strivings of some of the best of men; their highest intention is something other than to reward all men who are good, and a man who finds his plans frustrated by divinity need not conclude that his goals were therefore impious or immoral in addition to being contrary to divine plans. Sophocles represented the final victory of the gods as beautiful and ultimately to man's best interests; the benefits of the divine interventions, however, are usually remote and obscure. Above all, there is no obvious benefit in this life for the god's innocent victim himself. Troy needs the innocent suffering of Philoctetes, Salamis that of Ajax, Athens that of Oedipus, *we* need the heroes, and the martyrs are memorable and thrilling to watch. We are thankful for the innocent suffering of these heroes in some obscure way. But we cannot actually learn anything from them as to why we should be good. Or at least we cannot learn what some of Sophocles' contemporaries thought was the first premise of any moral system, that the reason why one should be truly excellent is that only then can one be truly free.

The Stoics had every reason to call Socrates their most important predecessor, at least in one respect. Socrates was the first to argue that complete freedom in the classical sense was really quite possible to achieve if one were intelligent enough. That is, the gods are humane in their demands and nature is benign, so a man who does the wisest of the things possible for him to do at every turn will in fact inevitably achieve lasting happiness, no matter how ill-advised and unjust the actions of other men toward him might be. But Socrates' was only the most startling and influential suggestion in what was really a prolonged and articulate debate. It may be that there never had been, and never has been since, a crisis in morality that was so brilliantly and so variously talked about by those living through it. Sometimes the debate centered on the scale of values received from society (was conventional morality a trap to take away your freedom? could you be free only if you were a *tyrannos*? will a shrewd man always circumvent the demands of his society?), sometimes on the role of the gods (are men's laws divinely inspired and administered or is there a superhuman code that cuts across men's laws? is this superhuman code liberating and really more humane than laws framed by mortals or is it something impossible for men to live by and be happy?).

Hard as it is to extract any logical argument from the plays of Sophocles (far harder than in the case of Aeschylus or Euripides), some things can be inferred about his stand in the debate about freedom: (1) The gods use the excellence of some men to bring benefits to mankind, or to certain cities or families, anyhow. (2) The most beneficial of human lives are not those which are enriched with happiness, but those full of innocent suffering. (3) The innocent suffering is contrived not by unjust men, but by the gods themselves; and the pious onlooker, the one who stands to benefit from the catastrophe, is he who realizes the godsent, involuntary nature of the pollution incurred by the sufferer. (4) The gods need not be thought of as bringing about involuntary pollution by ordering a good man to do something contrary to his nature, as Aeschylus thought; they sometimes allow him to act voluntarily on good motives and then make a mockery of the voluntary nature of what he had done by showing that he had not had some crucial piece of information. (5) Freedom can be won, therefore, neither in Socrates' nor the sophists' way, or at least this freedom is not guaranteed by the gods; they choose good men, not bad, to be the martyrs for the world.

What Oedipus is shown doing on the stage, hunting the killer of Laius, attempting to find out the identity of his parents, and so on: even this has an element of the involuntary in it. That is, the gods know, but he does not, that the outcome of his efforts is going to be stupefyingly different from what he could possibly guess. We hardly think about that, however; what occupies us most is Oedipus's discovery of what he had done involuntarily in the past, to his parents and to himself. We are watching a man come to the realization that he was, and had been for many years, although he did not know it, one of the chosen of the gods. By dramatizing the discovery instead of the innocent acts themselves, Sophocles has sharpened to an incredible degree the bitterness of being such a chosen one, the folly of supposing that a man can be free by being good. We may well ask why such a vision stirs us rather than depressing us or disgusting us as it did some of the Socratics, but we ought not to deny that this *is* the implication of the action we are watching.

Instead of saying that since the *Oedipus* moves us, therefore Oedipus must be a free agent, we should do better to say that since the *Oedipus* moves us, and he is obviously *not* free, the assumption that only the actions of a free agent could engage our deepest sympathies and interest ought to be looked at again. We should at least not close the debate before it is begun.

Illusion and Truth
in *Oedipus Tyrannus*

Karl Reinhardt

In contrast to the static scenic form of the earlier plays, we have seen that practically every scene of the *Antigone* portrays a reversal, which entails the development of a situation into its opposite. The *Oedipus Tyrannus,* taken as a whole, constitutes a reversal of the same kind, but on a larger scale, the scale of the whole drama. Of course the fall of kings from their power and glory was nothing new to the Athenian stage. But what a difference from the downfall of kings in Aeschylus, in the *Agamemnon* and the *Persians*! Aeschylus prepares for the coming event from the beginning. What anxiety in hope, what presentiments and affirmations from the choruses! What forebodings in the dialogue, how the downfall lies in wait in every word from the very beginning! And in Sophocles too, in the earlier *Trachiniae,* we could see how the tone imparted a presentiment of the approaching ruin, how the gloomy note struck by the very first words foretold it and prepared its way. And what a difference in the case of the *Oedipus Tyrannus,* where the beginning and the end, both of equal power and breadth, stand in contrast to each other! The beginning holds up one example, and the end another. At the beginning, a man who is everyone's shield and protection, at the end a man who is cast out from everywhere and everything, even from his share of the light. Between the two states there develops the play of the daimonic constellations as they glide forward, no longer separate, sharply divided, independent entities as they still were in the

From *Sophocles*. © 1979 by Basil Blackwell Publishers Ltd.

Antigone, but in a single movement, which begins slowly, then rushes with ever-increasing speed into a whirlpool of motion.

Little as we know of Aeschylus's *Oedipus,* we may nevertheless conclude that it did not portray this kind of reversal. That play formed the central section of the trilogy which Aeschylus produced in 467, where it was flanked by the *Laius* and the extant *Seven against Thebes.* Now, since in the *Seven against Thebes* the grandson falls victim to the family curse inherited from his father and grandfather, the *Oedipus* of Aeschylus must have had a different approach and a different tone. Moreover a dramatic technique involving *development,* which alone makes Sophocles' *Oedipus* possible, is still quite unknown in the *Seven against Thebes.*

To complete the contrast between the beginning and the end, to show before the uprooting both the roots and the soil from which this royal tree is to be torn—roots of such strength that their uprooting comes near to being an uprooting of all human foundations—Oedipus appears at the beginning not as what he had once been in the saga, the son of Tyche, the lucky man favoured by fortune who comes and wins a kingdom, but as the man blessed by grace, leader, helper, saviour, the regal figure sustained by the favour of the gods, who stands not for himself but for all, and who speaks on behalf of all. Furthermore, to add to his stature and increase his greatness, he is surrounded by a procession of suppliants who are in awe of him as though he were a god: by aged priests and also by a crowd of boys, so that his speech, which is addressed to them, begins like that of a father:

> OEDIPUS: Children, young sons and daughters of old
> Cadmus . . .
> What do you fear or want, that you sit here
> suppliant? Indeed I'm willing to give all
> that you may need; I would be very hard
> should I not pity suppliants like these.

The tone and attitude of this opening are taken up and carried on in continuing waves, as it were, by the solemn petition of the priest of Zeus:

> PRIEST: You see our company around the altar;
> you see our ages; some of us, like these,
> who cannot yet fly far, and some of us

heavy with age

. . . .
We have not come as suppliants to this altar
because we thought of you as of a God,
but rather judging you the first of men
in all the chances of this life and when
we mortals have to do with more than man . . .
In virtue of no knowledge we could give you,
in virtue of no teaching; it was God
that aided you, men say, and you are held
with God's assistance to have saved our lives.

(l. 15ff.)

Sophocles has here achieved a kingliness of diction matched only by Aeschylus in the *Agamemnon*. In the strains of the royal speech in the *Agamemnon* there is sublime knowledge of the forces of fate which hover around the royal power, but here in the *Oedipus* the words are those of a king bound by an inherited public obligation:

I know you are all sick
yet there is not one of you, sick though you are,
that is as sick as I myself.
Your several sorrows each have single scope
and touch but one of you. My spirit groans
for city and myself and you at once.

(l. 59ff.)

The first breach of the security of this situation does not come, as the saga might lead one to expect, from a reminder of the old Delphic oracle given at the birth of the outcast, which said that he would kill his father and violate his mother. On the contrary, very much in contrast with the role of the old prophecy in the *Trachiniae,* the oracle is kept well away from the opening of the play and is not mentioned until security has already been shattered and trust already broken—not until the quarrels with Tiresias and Creon. The first attack comes rather from a new directive from the Delphic god, to purify the land from the pollution caused by the blood of Laius—i.e. not from an oracle belonging to the saga but from a directive such as Delphi frequently issued in historical times. It set the searcher the task of finding himself. The task, no sooner set than performed, pervades the solver and soon begins to transform him, to bewitch him like a draught of some potion, to become for him a test of his existence. He is seized by an overwhelming desire to pledge himself, to discover—even before the return of Creon, who had been sent to consult the oracle:

> OEDIPUS: But when he comes, then may I prove a villain,
>   if I shall not do all the God commands.
>
> (l. 76ff.)

And even more as soon as Creon enters:

> OEDIPUS: What is the word you bring us from the God?
> CREON: A good word—for things hard to bear themselves
>   if in the final issue all is well
>   I count complete good fortune.
> OEDIPUS: What do you mean?
>   What you have said so far
>   leaves me uncertain whether to trust or fear.
> CREON: If you will hear my news before these others
>   I am ready to speak, or else to go within.
> OEDIPUS: Speak it to all;
>   the grief I bear, I bear it more for these
>   than for my own heart.
>
> (l. 86ff.)

Thus, from the very beginning, Oedipus is the mighty revealer, open in every gesture and every word, the same Oedipus who at the end shouts for the doors to be torn open so that all the world may see him.

But the suspense for which this play is famous is not maintained simply by the unrelenting breathlessness of a discovery which comes in regular stages, nor simply by the cat-and-mouse game played by a fate lying hidden in the past upon a victim who as yet suspects nothing, nor by an interplay of deceptions such as occurs in an interrogation or in the course of a trial—in short, not by any of the devices with which so many subsequent dramas of revelation have been crammed. Schiller referred to the *Oedipus* as a "tragic analysis" (a phrase which has been quoted far too often since), and said "Everything is there already and has only to be unravelled . . . Furthermore, what happens is far more terrifying in its nature because it is inevitable" (letter to Goethe, 2 October 1797). But he was looking at the play from the point of view of his own work on his *Wallenstein,* and was concerned too much with the mechanics of construction and too little with the essential. For Sophocles, as for the Greeks of an earlier age, fate is in no circumstances the same as predetermination, but is a spontaneous unfolding of daimonic power, even when the fate has been foretold, and even when it is brought about by means of an order immanent in events and in the way that the world goes. Fate as predetermination does not exist before the Stoa and the victory of astrology. So too the essential basis of the *Oedipus* is not the irrevocability of a past as revealed in the course of the play—there is no place in the *Oedipus* for the concept "Even if it were possible, I could no longer do what I wished." On the contrary, it is an actively pursued struggle for escape, self-assertion and defence on the part of a threatened world of illusion, a world which is human—indeed inextricably conjoined with an essentially human greatness; and from the point of view of this world and of its order, its "truth" and its preservation, the boundaries between reality and illusion have to be reversed. The *Oedipus* is by no means distinct from other Greek tragedies in being *the* tragedy of human fate, of which it has ranked for so long as prime example—taking "fate" as in the period of classicism in Germany as being inseparable from "liberty," the liberty "which elevates" at that. It would be much nearer the truth to say that it is distinct from other Greek tragedies in being *the* tragedy of human illusion, in which illusion implies reality, just as Parmenides' *Doxa* implies *Aletheia*. It should have struck critics before now that not one of all the choruses in the *Oedipus* sings about fate, though enough sing about it elsewhere, whereas one chorus in a prominent position sings about human "illusion":

> What man, what man on earth wins more
> of happiness than a seeming
> and after that turning away?
>
> (l. 1189ff.)

The fight and the defence on the part of illusion begin at first unobtrusively, but certainly as early as the start of the investigation ordered by the god. It begins with a strange diversion rightly observed but wrongly criticized by the logical Voltaire. After an enquiry into the facts seems already to have been planned, after the question "Is there a witness?" has already been asked, and after this question has been answered in the affirmative—the word "robbers" is heard, which suddenly arouses suspicion, supplanting the idea of an inquiry: how would robbers have dared to do that if they had not been bribed "from here"? "From here" would mean from some quarter in Thebes. The question, put after the murder of a king and by a king, is understandable. The question is addressed to Creon. Creon seems to evade it: the suspicion which naturally arose could not, he says, be followed up after the deed. Why not? The Sphinx came. With that the suspicion seems to rest for a while. But from now on, attention is directed not toward the scene of the deed, nor the course of events, nor the weapon, but toward the instigators, in Thebes—until suddenly, after the argument with the refractory and apparently malevolent prophet, the suspicion is confirmed, the link between Creon and Tiresias is established and a whole web of conspiracy stands confirmed as certain truth.

A fragment of Aeschylus's *Oedipus* happens to have survived (the only extant fragment, in fact) in which a witness, obviously the sole survivor, tells us of the "place where three roads meet." That must have been followed by the revelation, or a part of the revelation. In Sophocles there is no such interrogation in the whole play. The fragment of Aeschylus is enough to show what it was that Sophocles displaced by his diversion and its consequences, so as to make room for other things.

For as a result of this diversion, the original, inevitable and, so to speak, innate illusion is joined by a new illusion in the shape of a delusion. And the way in which this new illusion is introduced, in the form of a suspicion of bribery and a secret conspiracy within the city against which it is directed, shows the influence upon the *Oedipus* of the dramatic and scenic form of the *Antigone* and the outward cloak by means of which illusion took control of the figure of Creon in that play. There the suspicion of bribery was at first only hinted at by a single word—κέρδος (l.222)—only to be pushed aside by intervening matters, and then it suddenly appeared fully fledged, to be expanded in the scene with the seer. So too in the *Oedipus*. Except that in the *Antigone* the suspicion had already been suggested to the new ruler by the outward state of affairs when he took over, after the death of the heir to the throne and shortly after the defeat of the exile. In that play, the suspicion already lay hidden in the first proclamation, prohibiting the burial of the enemy of the country. In the *Oedipus,* the ruler makes his entrance before his people as a man universally honoured, surrounded by all his subjects and warmly greeted by them—not announcing his own arrival like Creon—so that the threat hardly seems to have any foundation in the outward situation. And yet here too there is the same suspicion, at first not directed at any particular person, which hovers until it settles, by way of Tiresias, on Creon. In other words, in the *Oedipus* the threat enters the human, subjective sphere, presses into the domain of the spirit, is sensed and felt from the daimonic incomprehensibility of the task rather than deduced from the outward circumstances. And the suspicion is attached to the wrong person because the victim of illusion must have an enemy, a tangible enemy, so as not to lose his own sense of security. For Creon the transgression of his prohibition did not in itself signify any danger to his own existence; for Oedipus everything is in the balance, even before he begins to guess what he stands to lose: his realm of illusion, which sees itself threatened, not at this stage by reality, but only by the illusory products of its own creation:

> OEDIPUS: For when I drive pollution from the land
> I will not serve a distant friend's advantage,
> but act in my own interest. Whoever
> he was that killed the king may readily
> wish to dispatch me with his murderous hand.
>
> (l. 137ff.)

The irruption of truth—one can hardly speak of reality in this context, since Oedipus does not at first live in illusion but in a world of objective falsity and appearance—the irruption of truth into the structure of appearance occurs from two successive breaches in the wall, the first at the edge, the second in the center. The first breach follows from the question "What is this hidden thing that confronts me, which it is my duty to bring into the open?"; the second from the question "What am I, and what is my own true existence?" For a while the second question lies hidden behind the first, then both run parallel for a time, in secret harmony, and at the end they come together. Both times, the structure tries to preserve itself and throws its forces toward the point from which the threat comes.

The first defence against the enemy, who is as yet unknown, is the proclamation of outlawry, and, together with this proclamation, the curse. And Oedipus knows how to curse. He curses with the power that his position bestows on him. As soon as cursing takes hold of him he speaks the words which carry their own fulfilment, the words which are simultaneously public and personal; he curses with priestly dedication and at the same time as if with ruffled plumage. We need only look at the curses in Euripides, for example those of Theseus in the *Hippolytus,* to see how little contact Euripides has with this kind of speech and action. But an almost greater disappointment comes if one compares the fragment of the old epic, the *Thebais* (fr. 3), which has been preserved by chance: there, nothing at all of the curse comes through into the written word—the narrative says that "he cursed" and no more.

The clearer it becomes that the curse is directed at none other than the unwitting curser himself, the greater the force of the speech which calls down the curse becomes. Creon's curses in the *Antigone* were similarly directed against the speaker, but the effect of recoil in the *Oedipus* is far more pregnant with fate. This curse has in common with Creon's speeches in the *Antigone* the dynamic force of its acceleration: each has a gentle opening, and then the speech begins to hurtle along like a man who is in danger of falling victim to a delusion. And again there is a reversal between the first part and the last, though in the *Oedipus* it takes place not in the course of the dialogue but in the twisting movement of the curse-speech itself. The moderate tone with which the speaker began, promising impunity if the wrongdoer were to confess, disappears as soon as outlawry has been solemnly decreed; the power of the curse and denunciation itself takes control of the speaker, the more he himself is implicated in the riddle that he wants to solve:

> So I stand forth a champion of the God
> and of the man who died.
> Upon the murderer I invoke this curse—
> whether he is one man and all unknown,
> or one of many—may he wear out his life
> in misery to miserable doom!
> If with my knowledge he lives at my hearth
> I pray that I myself may feel my curse.
>
> (l. 244ff.)

After the opening, where the new king still stands outside the unknown and almost forgotten event, he finds himself becoming uncannily involved in things alien to himself, as if they were his own. Although he is unaware of the relationship, he is already making himself the son of his real father; in the daimonic sphere of illusion his own true nature has already magically seized upon him in anticipation of things to come. At the opening he speaks as an outsider:

> what I say to you, I say
> as one that is a stranger to the story
> as stranger to the deed. For I would not
> be far upon the track if I alone
> were tracing it without a clue. But now,
> since after all was finished, I became
> a citizen among you, citizens—
> now I proclaim to all the men of Thebes.
>
> (l. 219ff.)

He is just as much an outsider as he had been before:

> CREON: My lord, before you piloted the state
>   we had a king called Laius.
> OEDIPUS: I know of him by hearsay. I have not seen
>   him.
>
> (l. 103ff.)

But from being an outsider he begins to involve himself more and more intensely:

> Since I am now the holder of his office,
> and have his bed and wife that once was his,
> and had his line not been unfortunate
> we would have common children—(fortune leaped
> upon his head)—because of all these things,
> I fight in his defence as for my father,
> and I shall try all means to take the murderer
> of Laius the son of Labdacus
> the son of Polydorus and before him
> of Cadmus and before him of Agenor.
>
> (l. 258ff.)

He has ended by giving a complete list of the ancestors of the present representative of the family. That is how kings name their ancestors when taking an oath, as Xerxes does in Herodotus (7.11): "If I do not take revenge on the Athenians, let me not be called son of Darius, son of Hystaspes, son of Arsames, son of Ariaramnes, son of Teispes, son of Cyrus."

Indeed, both are cases of tragic irony—the apparent lack of blood relationship and the apparent adoption of the same (the true adoption comes only at the time of the catastrophe). But even though this is only an apparent adoption, despite all its stormy impetuosity which leaves behind everything that is merely material, it is not until this adoption that reality and appearance are irrevocably twisted and woven together. It is only from this grappling together, which is no longer external, no longer pragmatic, but daimonic, embracing the whole being, the soul itself and language itself, that there arises the tragedy of the man hurled down from his realm of appearance, a tragedy which is also the answer to the question: What would Oedipus be to us if he did not happen to be the son of Laius? or: How is the exceptional case in the legend made into the symbolic figure in the drama? The daimonic, continual and unconscious reaching over out of the realm of appearance into the realm of truth is the human element which was not supplied by the legend and had not been linked with the figure of Oedipus before Sophocles. This also forms the irony which is usually described in modern aesthetic theory by the inaccurate and overgeneralized technical term "tragic irony." For here it is not a case of the spectator knowing the truth while the character on the stage gropes in the dark, so that the character's speech bears a different meaning for the spectator, but it is a case of man standing in confusion between appearance and reality. Moreover, appearance and reality are not simply apportioned to stage and audience, or even the other way round; still less are they apportioned to the writer on the one hand and the world that he has created on the other: on the contrary, both of them are seen in each and every word and gesture of the confused hero. It is not the writer, making use of his own world of appearance or of theatrical appearances, but the invisible gods, operating in the background from their position of unattainable remoteness, who are playing games with human appearances.

After the secret, unconscious conflict which points to the future, another conflict breaks out in the Tiresias scene—an open conflict between truth and appearance. No longer is it a conflict between truth and error. If we speak of error we do not imply that error is inevitable, as it is here; it is not merely the intellect, but the whole structure of a man, both internal and external, that is at fault. Deianira in the *Trachiniae* found herself in a state of tragic error: something overcame her, and, as soon as she realized it, she felt remorse; in the same play when Heracles raged he was in a state of tragic error. Tragic error is something which overwhelms a man. But the world of tragic appearance in which Oedipus finds himself is without any doubt characteristic of deeper tragedy: it contains and conditions the human state from the beginning, including a man's nature and aims, and his role as king, husband, leader, protector; it is his power and security, it is everything which preserves him. In the *Antigone* Creon was driven into a position of falsehood and appearance; Oedipus *stands* in a world of appearances, and is hurled down from it.

There is something about the human vehicle, the vessel of truth, the seer Tiresias, which is hard to comprehend, and not only for Oedipus when he misinterprets him. Half of Tiresias is superhuman, half only too human; half of him possesses secret knowledge and is infallible, half of him is indecisive and forgetful, coming and yet anxious to go, concealing and yet revealing; he is half a capricious, irritable old man, half—in the midst of his anger—possessed of second sight; he is a walking enigma, "nursing the truth that makes him strong" (l. 356)—part of the whole mysteriousness and paradox in the prophetic admonition, "Neither speak nor hide," seems to be personified in him. The paradoxical nature of his character certainly goes beyond that of Tiresias in the *Antigone;* he represents a further development of the figure of the seer in the earlier work. There is no longer any need to point out his blindness, or the boy leading the blind leader of the blind; instead, it is the paradox of the prophetic phenomenon itself which speaks. It is the same paradox throughout, something which, seen only from the point of view of the character, is totally incompatible with itself: the fusion of a self-willed, limited existence with a daimonic influence from the world beyond—yet this fusion does not make the man unambiguously ecstatic, an instrument of the god, an inspired prophet. It is a paradox of the same kind which dominates everything in the last work of Sophocles' old age, and when it is intensified to an altogether inconceivable degree by the firmness and breadth with which the character is drawn, it takes control of the aged Oedipus. If the mystery of this paradox is still lacking in the *Antigone* it is easy to infer that it was still beyond the reach of Sophocles when he wrote that work.

In the Tiresias scene in the *Antigone,* the fear and respect of the beginning gave way at the end to mockery and accusation. It is the same here. But now the transition is more violent and the content less rational. The first great speech of Oedipus to Tiresias, which not only shows royal respect for the seer as a person but also bows before the mystery of his office, is simultaneously a sincere attempt to win him over and an expression of trust in him. Thus it already goes beyond the *Antigone* in its noble gesture:

> Tiresias, you are versed in everything,
> things teachable and things not to be spoken,
> things of heaven and earth-creeping things.
>
> (l. 300ff.)

In the *Antigone* the conflict amounted, more or less, to a warning, which was ignored, and an accusation, which was followed by
the revelation of the accuser, but it still took the rational form of an
argument about right and wrong, about *hybris* and *sophrosynē*. In
contrast, Oedipus comes up against a mysterious resistance in the
seer himself, an obscure refusal to obey, a barricade set up against the
means of salvation, the question on which everything hangs. And
instead of right and wrong, it is "light" and "darkness" which clash
and accuse each other in turn, the former developing from obscurity
at the beginning to an increasingly bright and evil clarity, and the
latter from readiness and receptivity to an increasingly passionate
deafness; each is carried along into new extremes by the other.

The conflict soon reaches its first peak:

OEDIPUS: You would provoke a stone! Tell us, you villain,
        tell us, and do not stand there quietly
        unmoved and balking at the issue.

> (l. 344ff.)

The attack on the resistance of the seer is combined with the
attack on the resistance of the enigma which from the beginning,
ever since the message came from Apollo, has secretly endangered
and threatened the world of appearance surrounding Oedipus:
Tiresias is accused of being an accomplice to the deed. And this
attack, like the verbal battles in the *Antigone,* brings with it a conflict
between two spheres. Just as in the Tiresias scene of the *Antigone* the
argument was about the word "profit," κέρδος, which had two
meanings, human salvation and the search for material advantage,
here too the argument is about an ambiguous word; but it is a much
fiercer argument, since it is about "truth" and "darkness." For one
speaker, "truth" and "light" mean something which he is conscious
of having done, something which he surveys, something which sub-
mits to his will and perception; to the other it is something which is
hidden and denied to him. For the former it falls within the human
sphere, for the other it forms the limits of the human sphere. From
an objective point of view, Tiresias and the audience know a fact of

which Oedipus can have no knowledge; to that extent the conflict is an example of tragic irony in the conventional sense. But from the point of view of a man's existence it is not a confrontation of knowledge and ignorance of a certain fact, but of one mode of existence and another: what is "light" for one is "darkness" for the other:

> TIRESIAS: I say you are the murderer of the king
>   whose murderer you seek . . .
> OEDIPUS: Do you imagine you can always talk
>   like this, and live to laugh at it hereafter?
> TIRESIAS: Yes, if the truth has anything of strength.
> OEDIPUS: It has, but not for you; it has no strength
>   for you because you are blind in mind and ears
>   as well as in your eyes.
> TIRESIAS: You are a poor wretch
>   to taunt me with the very insults which
>   every one soon will heap upon yourself.
> OEDIPUS: Your life is one long night so that you cannot hurt
>   me or any other who sees the light.
>
> (ll. 362, 368ff.)

The clarity in which Oedipus lives, which "nurses" him, which is in and around him, the same for him as for all who "see the light"—without the appearance of this clarity this conflict would be a dialectical conflict in the Euripidean manner. This is the kind of clarity which has to label everything that threatens its existence as "darkness."

The threat becomes more intense until the god is named:

> TIRESIAS: It is not fate that I should be your ruin,
>   Apollo is enough; it is his care
>   to work this out.
> OEDIPUS: Was this your own design
>   or Creon's?
>
> (l. 376ff.)

The threat from the god is immediately replaced by an equivalent threat from man, in order to maintain the structure of the world of appearances. It is true that there have been attempts to use external concrete associations to explain this association, which is however an association made within the framework of a human mind. And Sophocles certainly has at least some pragmatic motivations in his work: as we have already said, it was Creon who suggested consulting Tiresias. But it is only possible for something like this to be taken as grounds for suspicion at all because of the general frame of mind of the person in question; the frame of mind is the given factor, and once suspicion has flared up there is no further talk of external factors whatever. The mention of Apollo is the dividing line, after which illusion has to become delusion and blindness in order not to surrender. From a basis in the world of appearance there immediately springs a whole world and a whole world order of delusion: Creon, the seer and the deed—a strange combination! And indignation has found an object to attack. Passion unburdens itself in the gnomic apostrophe with which Oedipus addresses this world:

> OEDIPUS: Wealth, sovereignty and skill outmatching skill
>   for the contrivance of an envied life!
>   Great store of jealousy fill your treasury chests,
>   if my friend Creon, friend from the first and loyal,
>   thus secretly attacks me, secretly
>   desires to drive me out and secretly
>   suborns this juggling, trick-devising quack,
>   this wily beggar who has only eyes
>   for his own gains, but blindness in his skill.
>
> (l. 380ff.)

The threat develops into an essential part of a newly forming system—the past, too, is now dragged into service to support appearances: where was the seer's wisdom at the time of the Sphinx? But is this view of the world false? Is it not right? What would appearances be if they did not present their own appearance of truth? Creon in the *Antigone* also justified himself on the grounds of something which was not false in itself. But in that play the relation between general truth and the reality of the moment had something repulsive and mean about it; in this case the disparity belongs to Oedipus's nature; it is a necessary part of his self-assertion and self-justification.

Again, the reply of the Tiresias of the *Oedipus* has something in common with the prophetic speech of the Tiresias of the *Antigone*: both combine a prophecy of the future with an interpretation of the present:

TIRESIAS: Since you have taunted me with being blind,
    here is my word for you.
    You have your eyes but see not where you are
    in sin, nor where you live, nor whom you live with.
    Do you know who your parents are? Unknowing
    you are an enemy to kith and kin
    in death, beneath the earth, and in this life.
    A deadly-footed, double-striking curse,
    from father and mother both, shall drive you forth
    out of this land, with darkness on your eyes,
    that now have such straight vision.

(l. 412ff.)

"Where you live": the words "live," "settle" and so forth are favourite words at this stage to designate a place in the order of things, the place where a man's activity belongs. It is not to be taken as an affectedly mystical circumlocution for something which could be expressed by a single word; the meaning is not simply "Thebes is your home, Jocasta your mother," although that is factually true. Origin, dwelling-place and friends, or in other words "whence," "where" and "with whom," together form an expression of the whole of human existence; and in Sophocles, insofar as human existence is tragic, it is always embedded in its context by nature yet tragically isolated. But as things are in this case, the seer's vague phrases describe matters more accurately than more precise words would. "You do not know with whom . . ." is an interpretation of a set of circumstances. "You do not know that Jocasta is your mother" would only be enlightenment about a single fact. But the sense is: you think you belong, yet you are in fact alien to everything to which a man belongs. "Beneath" and "on the earth" are the two polar extremes which stand for the whole range of blood relationships, as in the prophecy in the *Antigone* (ll.)1068–73, where the totality of all nature is expressed by the phrases "above" and "below," "the living" and "the dead." The final condition which Tiresias prophesies will again be no more than the making perceptible of what Oedipus already is in his true nature, although this is not as yet apparent. It is only from the standpoint of the daimonic sphere, which first makes itself felt in the seer's enigmatic utterance, that the condition in which a man finds himself can be defined. With the enigmatic, vague element in the seer's speech, what was in the legend simply an unrolling of the action and a pressing forward into the future, is brought into the present, into existence, and placed as a truth in that world of appearances, that darkness, which is inseparably linked with Oedipus.

The next *epeisodion*, the clash between Oedipus and Creon, stands in contrast with the Tiresias scene in more or less the same way as the clash with Haemon does with the Tiresias scene in the *Antigone:* after the obscure, mantic world of darkness and the irrational, there enters the rational man, who sees that he too, in his own very different kind of stability, is threatened by the attack upon the seer. (Compare the two adjacent argument scenes in the *Ajax:* at that early stage there is hardly any contrast at all between them.) But the two argument scenes are now linked: the second is a continuation of the first. They take the action further and further from its objective, from the task of self-recognition, until we discover that what on the human level is a diversion leads, in the daimonic context, to the objective. That is how oracles usually reach their objective; they prefer roundabout paths, they tend to come true at the very moment at which a man seems to have escaped them. But here it is no longer a case of Sophocles' having taken over in his drama a few external, formal elements from archaic stories about oracles, as he did in the *Trachiniae;* instead, he has seized and dramatized the experience and the deeper human roots which give rise to the oracular detours. In the *Oedipus* the oracle is no longer, even formally, the lever of an action of the impetus towards a self-recognition as it was in the *Trachiniae*. Rather, it is the subsoil of the oracular, the roots which it strikes in the mind, which also serves as the ground from which the drama grows.

In the *Oedipus* there is no repetition of the continuous crescendo which characterized the argument scenes of the *Antigone*. Instead of developing from a position where both parties wrongly believe that they are in agreement, the argument is waged from the very beginning with great vehemence. One man storms on to the stage full of anger; the other soon clashes with his opponent in an even plainer state of fury. The static and immobile nature of the scene is shown by the parallel accusations, of equal violence, from each side. But this duel is different in nature from those in the *Ajax*—between them lies the phase of dramatic technique involving development which we saw in the *Antigone*. For the battle, stationary at first, soon begins to twist, to turn and to vacillate—it is a fight in which one opponent exhausts himself in reckless assaults, while the other parries his thrusts with a scientific defence. (That is why Creon has to appear on the stage first, so that Oedipus can come upon him):

> OEDIPUS: You, sir, how is it you come here? Have you so
> much brazen-faced daring that you venture in
> my house although you are proved manifestly
> the murderer of that man, and though you tried,
> openly, highway robbery of my crown?
>
> (l. 532ff.)

That is how he opens his attack. What had first arisen merely as a fleeting suspicion—the unexplained question of why the seer had said nothing after the deed and why the investigation was called off—is now turned against the enemy in what seems to be a successful investigation. But immediately after this first blow, the interrogator loses his lead in the *stichomythia* to Creon, the man under interrogation, who throws in a counterquestion which has the effect of a counterattack. In this his weapon is his rational lucidity, his knowledge of his own innocence and lack of guile. For him the fight is easy, for he has no deep roots, no lofty aspirations, and never reaches the borders of a superhuman sphere. He has no drives except those which he can consciously control and sensibly fulfil, no relationships except those which bring an "advantage" (τὰ σὺν κέρδει καλά), no qualities except those which can be calculated and entered on a "balance sheet." His "balance sheet," his λόγον διδόναι, may remind us of that of Euripides' Hippolytus (δοῦναι λόγον). But the difference is that in Euripides the balance, the *ratio,* is no longer shackled to the totality of man, but belongs to man's essential nature; man is divided into *ratio* and passion; whereas in the *Oedipus* the *ratio* serves only as an outside obstacle against which the truly human element can crash and break up. The figure of Creon who opposes the tragic victim represents the rational, enlightened *bios* of the age, all the more aware of himself for being on trial, neither capable of nor needing further self-knowledge through suffering, summing himself up: "This I am, that I am not; this, in consequence, I am capable of doing, that I am not capable of doing," and not making a single mistake about it. For there are such people, besides the tragic figures. Always, in the works of Sophocles, the great tragedy can be unfolded only against the background of the nontragic: that is why the generals and Odysseus stand in contrast with Ajax, Ismene with Antigone, the world of the watchman who saves his own skin in contrast with Antigone and her self-sacrifice . . . and this too is how Creon stands in contrast with Oedipus: in contrast with the leader, the ruler, the man of the highest aspirations, the first in all things, stands Creon, the man of faultless reputation who shrinks from every risk and danger to his own person, who protects himself, makes attachments, is satisfied with profit rather than power, is reasonable in a mediocre way, born to come second in everything. It is easy to see who wins: it is Creon, who gets the first halves of the lines and who has the last word before Jocasta separates the combatants. Oedipus is secretly wounded, bleeding internally from the consequences of his own blind charge against an opposition that stands its ground, rather than wounded by any particular verbal attack: at the end he is fighting only within his own enclosed world, he hardly sees whether his blows strike the target:

> OEDIPUS: When he that plots against me secretly
> moves quickly, I must quickly counterplot.
> If I wait taking no decisive measure
> his business will be done, and mine be spoiled.
>
> (l. 618ff.)

How well this would serve as a defence against Oedipus's conduct! How ill matched it is to the "balance sheet" to which it is the answer! The threat of the death penalty, too, is much more a burst of anger, a violent release of feeling, than a decision: it is as if the world of appearances in which Oedipus stands holds him fast and does not allow him to exercise any influence upon the world of reality. A threatened king, who could defend himself, a powerful man who in the end is left with nothing, is lost, and can only cry (l. 629), "O city, city!"

In the *Antigone* the opponents disagreed only to separate at the climax of their quarrel. In the *Oedipus* the disagreement is calmed down, almost lulled to peace by the short lines which the chorus exchange with the speaker and the influence of their rhythm on the stormy spirit. And no less soothing is Jocasta's entry into the quarrel between her brother and her husband. The last part of the *Ajax* has already given us an example of a quarrel which finishes in this way, with the entry of a third person who settles the matter. But here in the *Oedipus* we find that there has been a great development from the earlier type of scene. We have already noticed with regard to the external, technical aspect of the play that Sophocles has at last learnt to write a proper conversation for three characters. Indeed, one would look in vain in the *Trachiniae,* the *Ajax* or even the *Antigone* for an exchange such as we have here between Jocasta, Oedipus and Creon. But the real significance of achieving a dialogue for three actors lies in a change of style rather than in a mere technical advance. If we cast a glance at comedy, we find even in the earliest play of Aristophanes, the *Acharnians* of 425, written when he was still quite young, a succession and mixture of conversations and interchanges as varied as anyone could wish for even on the modern stage. So it was not an unprecedented achievement. But this achievement would have made no sense in a Sophoclean tragedy. For in Sophocles' plays, even at a later date, the purpose of the speeches is not to give details about the characters, or to establish the milieu, or even to give scope for conversation, as in nineteenth-century drama. Nor is there in Sophocles any society, or court, or anything like that, of the kind that sustains a conversation between several people in Shakespeare's early plays. Thus the first dialogue for three persons in the *Oedipus* is one of the signs of an individual style of scene-construction which Sophocles has only just achieved. In the *Ajax,* Odysseus intervened between the quarrelling heroes just as Jocasta intervenes between Oedipus and Creon. But the result was merely a dialogue between different pairs of speakers who took it in turns to confront each other; there was no true conversation *à trois.* The static confrontations by which the archaic type of emotional scene was presented would have been weakened, not strengthened, by a conversation between three persons. It is only in the interplay of shifting movements and changes, in a kind of emotional scene that does not stand still, but turns this way and that under the pressure of the daimon, that dialogue for three can express tragic content; for this form of dialogue, with its changing relationships, is itself one of transitions and transformations. Here, as always, it is the inner form which shapes the external form or, in other words, the technique. The arrival of the third person, and the appeasement she brings, does not in this case constitute a conclusion but a reversal, *a peripeteia;* not a sharp break but an ascent to the main peak of this unusually long *epeisodion* with all its twists and turns—an *epeisodion* which, in addition to the contrast of the large areas, also contains a wealth of transitions, half-lights and flickering intermediate states.

Although the accused gets away free, and anger releases its victim, this brings about not relief and ease but an even more oppressive anxiety. For now the anger is turned inwards, the wound festers under the scar. The victim of accusation, now set free, can say to his accuser, and obviously with justification:

> CREON: I see you sulk in yielding and you're dangerous
> when you are out of temper; natures like yours
> are justly heaviest for themselves to bear.
>
> (l. 673ff.)

When he has lost the certainty of his goal, the pursuit of the accuser turns into a new awareness that he himself is being hunted, and of a monstrous injustice of which he is the victim. The unity of the world without and the world within, of action and emotion, vanishes. The illusion which forms the basis of his certainty still exists, but it has already collapsed inwardly and been undermined subconsciously even before a convulsion from outside, starting from a point that had almost escaped notice, tears down the whole structure.

Anyone who considers that the accused is not guilty is heaping suspicion upon the royal accuser himself:

> OEDIPUS: I would have you know that this request of yours
> really requests my death or banishment.
>
> (l. 658f.)

There are the only possible alternatives, so certain is he of the guilt of the man he has accused. That is the extent to which the deluded Oedipus has staked his honour and rank on his mistake. Yet he is prepared, by releasing the man he supposes to be the traitor, to take upon himself another's guilt—established by his own deluded "either / or"; prepared to represent himself as the innocent victim of persecution and suffering so that he can bitterly reproach the other persons present:

> OEDIPUS: Well, let him go then—if I must die ten times for it,
> or be sent out dishonoured into exile.
>
> (l. 669f.)

What has happened? Logically it is absurd. But as Oedipus hovers between apportioning and accepting blame, wounded in his soul, his illusion shattered, he grasps the truth without realizing it, just as previously he had adopted his own family without realizing it. What first came into his mind as an "as if" now actually becomes reality. The daimonic does not invade it from outside except insofar as it has caused the anticipation of possibilities in Oedipus's own mind to make it receptive to a fate coming from outside.

Thus the turning-point is prepared, and truth forces its way in, no longer in the guise of a foreign enemy who presents a threat from the borders, but from the innermost center of the very core of his own being. And here again it begins with a state of transition, an uncertainty. Creon left. Will not Oedipus leave too? Will the queen not lead him away, fatally mistaken as he is? But she still has one question to ask: what has happened? When the chorus of old men, who are standing by, evades this question, she finally puts it to the stricken, silent Oedipus—who thereupon reveals himself, already almost more as a son would to his mother. Transitions such as this had never been known before.

The blood relationship is not spelt out in situations specially designed for it, but is more like a soft accompaniment which can be perceived in the tone of the words and the manner of address:

> OEDIPUS: Yes, I will tell you.
> I honour you more than I honour them.
>
> .   .   .   .
>
>   Whom
> should I confide in rather than you, who is there
> of more importance to me who have passed
> through such a fortune?
>
> (ll. 700, 772ff.)

She is the rescuer, he is the lost one. But the more assured Jocasta becomes in speaking words of comfort, the more precipitously Oedipus is plunged into despair. Like Creon's *hybris* in the *Antigone,* her words of comfort are summed up in a *gnomē,* in the form of a generalization (ll. 724–25): it is based on an enlightened belief in divinity. But as in the *Oedipus* the danger to man lies not in the *hybris* of human self-assertion but in the *hybris* of seeming as opposed to being that is innate in his nature—a deeper danger—, what is amiss in her attempt at consolation is not the arrogance of the individual will but the fact that the consolation is grounded in appearance and not in reality. Since the time of A. W. Schlegel it has been usual to speak confidently of Jocasta's "levity" or "blasphemy."

But what kind of pious respect could she be expected to accord to the belief that the oracle to which she had had to sacrifice her son had none the less come true? Has the sacrifice been in vain, the sacrifice that was her fate? And what good has that been to Laius? He has been murdered by robbers! Again, if Tiresias is asserting obvious impossibilities, is it "levity" for her not to believe in them? Is she "godless" because after this news her doubt is directed, not against the god himself, but only against his priest? After all that has happened, is she not, like Oedipus, living in an objective, necessary world of appearance? Her words are brief and definite (σημεῖα σύντονα), dispersing at a stroke, as she believes, the whole cloud of impossible suspicion which has gathered around him:

> JOCASTA: Do not concern yourself about this matter;
> listen to me and learn that human beings
> have no part in the craft of prophecy.
>
> . . . .
>
> So clear in this case were the oracles,
> so clear and false. Give them no heed, I say;
> what God discovers need of, easily
> he shows to us himself.
>
> (l. 707ff.)

The revelation, which in the *Oedipus* of Aeschylus came from outside, by means of an account given by an eyewitness, is shifted by Sophocles to an intimate scene in which two souls reveal themselves to each other. The monologue form, which was used in the *Trachiniae* when the tragic self-knowledge which sprang from the fulfilment of an oracle cried out in its agony to the world—the same monologue form which was used at the end of Aeschylus's *Seven against Thebes,* when Eteocles, Oedipus's son, recognizing the heritage of his blood, accepted his fate—has given way here in Sophocles' *Oedipus* to a movement to and fro, an exchange between souls driven onward by the daimon. Instead of moving in the manner of an emotionally charged messenger's speech, the narrative rushes along in staccato sentences, seeking relief under heavy pressure, with no room for decoration, no room for metaphors. (Contrast the language used in the revelation by Heracles in the *Trachiniae* (l. 1157ff.), the circumlocution for "not living, but dead" (l. 1160f.), the piling up of epithets to denote the holy place (l. 1167ff.), the emotive pleonasm of the phrase referring to the present (l. 1169), etc. There is nothing of this sort in the *Oedipus*.)

As in the *Trachiniae* (l. 1141), however, it is again the unintentional utterance of a *word* which leads to the revelation: in that play the word "Nessus," here "the place where three roads meet." The latter had already been named in a similar manner in the *Oedipus* of Aeschylus—the scholia on Sophocles' comment on the fact. But when it was named in Aeschylus, it was clothed in such a display of tragic splendour! It took three lines to strike the fateful note:

> We were coming on our way to the place where three
> highways part in branching roads, where we crossed
> the junction of the triple roads at Potniae.

In using an abundance of decorative epithets to convey pathos, Aeschylus does not scorn to double almost every expression. It is obvious that after this there could be no further questioning, corroboration, or doubt. There remained only the emotional unburdening of the hero as he saw the truth. (To attribute the surviving three lines to Oedipus himself instead of to an eyewitness would surely be to take too little account of their form.) In the *Trachiniae* (l. 1143ff.) the hero also comes to self-knowledge as soon as the fateful word has been uttered, apostrophizes himself and unburdens himself in a similar way; as indeed Eteocles had done before him in Aeschylus's *Seven against Thebes* (l. 640ff.) when he saw his father's curses being fulfilled. In Sophocles' *Oedipus* there is no apostrophe, no self-indulgent word, nothing left of the tragic unburdening which belonged to the older manner of expressing pathos. Instead there is an interplay of ignorance and apprehension, incomprehension and self-discovery, hesitation and certainty. For the first time the exchange of lines in the dialogue becomes the expression of an oscillation between salvation and destruction (how different from the monologues in the *Trachiniae*!), the expression of an uncomprehended fear, so paralysing that it scarcely dares to speak. The restrained emotion here is more effective than emotion which unburdens itself without restraint; the hesitating "maybe," "it seems," the word as yet unspoken, as yet unnamed, runs ahead of the clear revelation of the terrible truth, and in place of the earlier imagery and sound effects there appears the simple, unadorned movement of the dialogue:

OEDIPUS: I thought I heard you say
    that Laius was killed at a crossroads.
JOCASTA: Yes, that was how the story went and still
    that word goes round . . .
OEDIPUS: What have you designed, O Zeus, to do with me?
JOCASTA: What is the thought that troubles your heart?
OEDIPUS: Don't ask me yet—tell me of Laius—
    How did he look? How old or young was he?
JOCASTA: He was a tall man and his hair was grizzled
    already—nearly white—and in his form
    not unlike you.
OEDIPUS: O God, I think I have
    called curses on myself in ignorance.
JOCASTA: What do you mean? I am terrified
    when I look at you.
OEDIPUS: I have a deadly fear
    that the old seer had eyes.
    If it happened there was any tie
    of kinship twixt this man and Laius—

                                  (l. 729ff.)

Here at last the man and the woman are clearly seen to be united in their involvement in the same fate. But even closer than this visible unity is their unseen unity: they are both fighting to preserve the same world of appearance, which at one and the same time links and divides them; and when one of them stumbles, the same action or word makes the other imagine that he is standing all the more firmly. For this scene is the reversal of the one that follows. First Jocasta believes herself and Oedipus to be safe, just when he is falling headlong into the truth as though into a chasm; and similarly Oedipus struggles up again into his world of appearance and thinks that he can save himself, just when Jocasta is falling headlong into her part of the truth.

For what has begun to be revealed is still only half of the truth; and, because it is only half, it allows the structure built by belief to seem even more precarious at first than it did when appearances held full sway. The half-demolished world of illusion stands within the half-truth like an overhanging building of which part has collapsed. But Oedipus, still terrified by the collapse, is already at work propping up what is still standing, by prayer, by intelligence, by will-power, by his readiness to flee, from Thebes, from Corinth, from every danger that threatens (l. 824ff.).

One hope remains, weak though it is: the hope of preserving his world of appearance, which, from man's point of view, is the same as preserving his very existence. While everything around him is calculated to bring him insight into his deed and himself, there remains a contradiction in the number! The number—for according to the account of the eyewitness, several men were responsible for the death of Laius; indeed, because of the contradiction in the number it has been suggested that the whole of the *Oedipus* is built on a trick. As though the number were not merely something to which illusion can cling! and as though every illusion, on the point of sinking beneath the water, did not reach out to find something to hold on to! Is it contrary to human nature for a man to cling with all his intelligence to a hope, however faint, and argue desperately on the strength of it? For in such cases intelligence is guided by instinct. And is it contrary to human nature for a woman, with her more powerful instinct, to try to drive her intelligence more violently and forcibly than a man?

> JOCASTA: Be sure, at least, that this was how he told the
> story. He cannot unsay it now, for every one in the
> city heard it—not I alone. But, Oedipus, even if he
> diverges from what he said then, he shall never
> prove that the murder of Laius squares rightly with
> the prophecy—for Loxias declared that the king
> should be killed by his own son. And that poor
> creature did not kill him surely,—for he died him-
> self first. So far as prophecy goes, henceforward I
> shall not look to the right hand or the left.
>
> (l. 848ff.)

It is not that, as has been suggested, Jocasta's "levity" has increased in the meantime—it is surely too much to ask that she should make distinctions between god and prophet at this point; the difference between this and what she said earlier in the same *epeisodion* is rather that instead of the voice of unquestioned certainty that we heard previously, we now hear a most vehement defence. Here, in the guise of ingenious argument, is Jocasta's defence of her very existence, the feminine will to live and to preserve, for the man's sake, rather than any inadequacy of character. It remains true that this leads to *hybris* in the face of the gods. But if this is true, it is much rather because it springs from the roots of human nature itself than because it belongs to the particular nature of one particular human being.

If proof were still needed that doubt and reason are here nothing but means of defence, weapons used by an existence which feels itself to be threatened, and are not to be confused with the attitude of the freethinkers in the age of the Sophists, then it is provided by the beginning of the third *epeisodion,* when Jocasta offers prayers and sacrifice to the very same Lycean Apollo (whose image stands next to the door of the house) whose oracle she has doubted. For now she feels fear, even if not in herself and for herself, a terrible fear nevertheless: fear of Oedipus's fear:

> JOCASTA: not conjecturing,
>   like a man of sense, what will be from what was,
>   but he is always at the speaker's mercy,
>   when he speaks terrors.
>
> (l. 915ff.)

But instead of unburdening herself of her distress in loud lamentation or in pleas, as she might have done in a scene in Sophocles' earlier style—in the way that, for example, Tecmessa or Deianira unburdened themselves—her sacrifice is followed by a silence; and into this silence, with an incredible effect of an intrusion from the world outside, comes the messenger with the news of the death of Polybus. According to the laws of the earlier style, to which the *Ajax* and the *Trachiniae* still conform, some warning of this new element should have been given before it entered. But here something completely strange suddenly rushes in: it is the daimon cutting across the action with an irony very similar to that with which the watchman in the *Antigone* interrupted Creon's pronouncement. Jocasta has scarcely turned to pray—when lo and behold, by chance, yet miraculously, and quite independently of her volition, there enters something which appears to put an end to all her troubles as though by divine command:

> JOCASTA: O oracles of the Gods, where are you now? It
>   was from this man Oedipus fled, lest he should be

his murderer! And now he is dead, in the course of
nature, and not killed by Oedipus.

(l. 946ff.)

There now begins a series of developments which it has long
been customary to compare with moves in a game of chess. But even
this outward interplay of circumstances, some of which are introduced artificially, plays its particular part in the whole, and sheds its
particular light in the general gloom, only because it unrolls in an
atmosphere of spiritual breakdown, against a background of inner
confusion. Two-thirds of the play, in fact nearly all of it, is already
over, before the outer constellation of the facts impinges upon the
inner constellation, that of the spiritual conflicts. For everyone who
has joined Oedipus on the stage up to this point—Creon, Tiresias or
Jocasta—has basically been no more than an expression, result, helper
or hindrance of Oedipus's own searching, straying, and illusion, and
has joined him only to the extent that Oedipus's own illusion called
for it and came forward to meet it. But now the action of messengers
from distant cities, and the introduction of events, some very recent,
some from long ago, form a barrier of linked chains around the
turmoil of Oedipus's spirit. And how clearly Sophocles shows that
this element is introduced from outside! The good old messenger
reels from shock to shock: it is not the news that Oedipus has inherited the throne of Corinth but the news of the death of Polybus
which is regarded as almost incredible, has to be proved point by
point, and unleashes jubilation as though it brought relief from dire
distress. And soon he is even less certain of what confronts him; he
hesitates—shall he or shall he not? But it is his own good fortune that
it is the king's greatest good fortune to learn from his lips that he is
not the dead man's son! So as the bearer of good news he is brought
into the conversation as a third person, and his account swells with
the happiness of an old man who has at last been allowed to reveal
how he rescued the king as a foundling—so that in his joy he does
not even notice that he has changed his solemn mode of address:

Son,
it's very plain you don't know what you're doing.

(l. 1008)

A homely expression like "very" in the Greek here would still
have been impossible in, for example, the *Trachiniae,* in spite of the

lengthy dealings with messengers in that play; the style ruled it out. For the representation of pathos in that play still gave no hint of any ironic contrasts between outward events and inner suffering, so that a clash between them could not be mirrored in the language. On the other hand, the representation of the lower orders is another point of resemblance between the *Oedipus* and the *Antigone*.

The contrast between the two old people who rescued Oedipus as a child, one happily pressing forward, the other suddenly afraid and holding back, echoes in the tones of the common people the contrast between the two main tragic figures as they come to recognize themselves:

> HERDSMAN: Not such that I can quickly call to mind.
> MESSENGER: That is no wonder, master. But I'll make
> him remember what he does not know. For I
> know, that he well knows the country of
> Cithaeron, how he with two flocks, I with one kept
> company for three years—each year half a year—
> from spring until autumn time and then when
> winter came I drove my flocks to our fold home
> again and he to Laius' steadings. Well—am I right
> or not in what I said we did?
> HERDSMAN: You're right—although it's a long time ago.
> MESSENGER: Do you remember giving me a child to bring
> up as my foster child?
> HERDSMAN: What's this? Why do you ask this question?
> MESSENGER: Look old man, here he is—here's the man who
> was that child!
> HERDSMAN: Death take you! Won't you hold your tongue?
> OEDIPUS: No, no, do not find fault with him, old man.
> Your words are more at fault than his.
> HERDSMAN: O best of masters, how do I give offence?
> OEDIPUS: When you refuse to speak about the child of whom
> he asks you.
> HERDSMAN: He speaks out of his ignorance, without
> meaning.
>
> (l. 1131ff.)

The contrast between the two old men who give evidence here, one in fear and the other in joy, one denying and the other convicting himself, is quite different from the contrast between the messengers in the play of intrigue in the *Trachiniae*. What this interplay added to the main tragedy in the *Trachiniae*—in which a messenger was similarly convicted of deception, and there was a similar incongruity between the noble dignity of the task entrusted and the vulgarity of the man to whom it was entrusted—was only the questionable nature of human relationships: false appearance and presumptuous though well-meaning deception could not prevail. In the *Oedipus* the two messengers are indeed in themselves, in their fears and expectations, good, honest, even if self-centered, servants, but in the context of the whole merely unwitting, ignoble instruments of divine fate. The irony which sets them in contrast is the irony of the intrigue by which the divine will interweaves higher and lower things in order to manifest itself in the instability of human greatness.

Structurally, the third *epeisodion* is also divided into two. First it climbs steadily from fear to a gasp of relief, the victory of certainty— here Jocasta is the leader; and then, with a sudden new wave of anxiety, it climbs again from fear to certainty—but this time Oedipus is the leader and Jocasta counterbalances him in her fall, her entreaties and her final departure. But there is also an inner reversal between the beginning and the end. At first it was Oedipus who could not shake off his fear, and Jocasta who urged him to trust to "fortune," "chance," life in whatever form it presents itself (εἰκῆ κράτιστον ζῆν, where εἰκῆ means, not "frivolously," but disregarding the mysterious and obscure, not opening up the depths which make life problematic, for it is the gods who make man problematic): soon it is Oedipus who, taking refuge in his world of appearance for the last time, calls himself the "son of fortune," at the very moment that Jocasta despairs of him and her life is torn from the rock to which it clings. Her action at this point has already been foreshadowed in the *Trachiniae* (l. 815) when Deianira, suddenly breaking off and leaving the others in error about herself, made her exit. In that play too the chorus had made questionable conjectures and had been rebuked for it. But whereas in the *Trachiniae* the scene had been cast in the form of narrative report typical of the old style, filled throughout with the sustained emotion of the speaker, here Jocasta herself is seized and expelled by her own daimon, which sinks and rises, soars and collapses. And just as her disappearance signifies her fall from a false sense of security, so too the misunderstanding that she leaves behind her is disproportionately more cruel and ironic than that to which Deianira fell victim: in Deianira's case the mis-

understanding consisted only of the misinterpretation of quiet actions and a noble nature; here, in the *Oedipus,* it is an ironic outburst
of the daimonic latent within the person, a monstrous error spring-
ing from an innate obsession with a world of appearance—for at the
same time the world of appearance establishes itself in its own ruins,
as if it were fashioning a new, final vehicle of deception out of its
own broken timbers:

> CHORUS: I am afraid that trouble
> will break out of this silence.
> OEDIPUS: Break out what will! I at least shall be
> willing to see my ancestry, though humble.
> Perhaps she is ashamed of my low birth,
> for she has all a woman's high-flown pride.
> But I account myself a child of Fortune,
> beneficent Fortune, and I shall not be
> dishonoured. She's the mother from whom I spring;
> the months, my brothers, marked me, now as small,
> and now again as mighty. Such is my breeding,
> and I shall never prove so false to it,
> as not to find the secret of my birth.
>
> (l. 1074ff.)

In the *Ajax,* deception arises from insanity sent by the god; it is
something external to the man, something interposed by fate against
the course of nature; it is this deception which, through the power of
the god, crushes the hero's existence; he does not bring about his
own destruction. In the Deianira-drama of the *Trachiniae* the pitiful
mistake comes with Deianira's loss of normal awareness when her
grief-laden, fearful, loving spirit is troubled. In the *Oedipus,* deception is something in the atmosphere, something hovering around,
the daimonic fate in the nature and surroundings of Oedipus himself.
Although these different degrees of failure to recognize the truth do
not form a progression, it is not easy to imagine them in any other
sequence, or to regard the much more limited tragedy of recognition
in the *Trachiniae* as the more mature.

The last two short *epeisodia* of the action are richer in movement
than any other even in Sophocles. But even the final contrast of the final
rise and fall would never have been possible were it not for the contrast
of the two human lives here sinking to their ruin, and the deeply felt
contrast between the woman's attitude to fate and the man's. For *she*

is made to fear or to hope not by truth in itself, not by the true situation, but by the man she loves, by his situation and his moods. In security or fear, her relationship with the truth is *indirect,* but her relationship with life and instinct is all the more *direct*—even her good sense is instinctual. Whereas Oedipus acts with "pathos," in the original sense of suffering, she acts with sym-pathy in the same sense. That is why she also outdoes him in joy and hope, when she is triumphant, to the point of *hybris,* and when she collapses, to the point of self-destruction. Thus she counts it as victory if he can only begin to hope again, even though his hope is vain, and her final defeat lies not in seeing her own true position but in seeing how he will see his:

> JOCASTA: I beg you—do not hunt this out—I beg you,
>   if you have any care for your own life.
> What *I* am suffering is enough. . . .
>
> O Oedipus, God help you!
> God keep you from the knowledge of who you are!

Is Jocasta really to be characterized as "a frivolous woman"? Hardly. For it is only the difference between the two centers of existence, those of Jocasta and Oedipus, and the difference between their relationship to life, that makes possible the interaction, cross-currents and the intensification of the tragic waves which roll through the last part of the *Oedipus. Her* monstrous fault, which springs from *her* distress, is her readiness to accept even this last illusion, even if it remains no more than an illusion, for the sake of life, his life. Similarly, *his* monstrous fault is to accept even such a life—the life of a blinded, accursed man—if only it is the truth. The real action does not lie in the chess-like moves of their external fates, but in their reception of the truth as it impinges upon two different types of nature and behaviour. Therefore, although the breakthrough to recognition had already taken the same form in the fate of Heracles in the *Trachiniae* as it now does in the *Oedipus,* nevertheless the self-recognition attained by Heracles still remains within the confines of his preoccupation with himself, insofar as it is no more than recognition of his own approaching death; for even if Heracles does rise out of it to perform his last act as a conqueror, he still fails, in his finite, limited existence as a hero, to see himself as he is. Thus in his case even the sudden light of recognition takes the form of self-address, self-pity and sorrowful subjectivity:

HERACLES: Woe, woe is me! This is my miserable end.
  Lost! I am lost! I see the light no longer.

  (l. 1143f.)

But in the case of Oedipus the recognition no longer takes the form of an expression of his own pain, felt only by himself. While his pain is by no means diminished as a result, Oedipus's recognition sums up a total existence of, as it were, universal validity:

HERDSMAN: But he saved it
  for the most terrible troubles. If you are
  the man he says you are, you're bred to misery.

OEDIPUS: O, O, O, they will all come,
  all come out clearly! Light of the sun, let me
  look upon you no more after today!
  I who first saw the light bred of a match
  accursed, and accursed in my living
  with them I lived with, cursed in my killing.

  (l. 1180ff.)

The language is no longer the elevated language used by Heracles in the *Trachiniae,* rich in powerful images, exclamations, and enumerations of his own sufferings; instead, we find here a restraint, for instead of exaggerated gesture at a moment of pathos there is a single image (not for mere decoration but a true image of the sense), and instead of underlining of too obvious a kind we find a sort of litotes—a litotes of gestures that are left to convey their own meaning. Similarly it can be seen that in the final narrative, which again has many features in common with the final narrative of the *Trachiniae* (l. 900ff.), although the pathos is by no means diminished in the *Oedipus,* its significance is now not so much confined to the pathos itself, as an expression of pain; rather the pathos is filled with a more general significance, and thus it is able to express the actual tragic content. I do not mean the kind of gnomic summing-up which we find everywhere at the conclusion or opening of a speech, but the universal significance of the whole. It is true that in the material of the *Trachiniae* everything is already much more limited and more intimate, but the powerful public and universal significance of the last part of the *Oedipus* does not signify any lack or shortage of some element present in the *Trachiniae,* but only that its character as a general moral example outweighs its interest as an individual case. We no longer have a story with its own beginning, its own end, its own reversal, presenting an emotional shock in all its details, as in the *Trachiniae* (l. 900ff.), no longer a narrated drama for the second act and continuation of an acted drama, as in the *Antigone* (l. 1205ff.), but the end of what is already visible, forcing its way out into the gestures and accusations of the blinded man who at last can see:

> SECOND MESSENGER (speaking of Jocasta): she went
>   straight to her marriage bed, tearing her hair
>   with both her hands, and crying upon Laius
>   long dead—Do you remember, Laius,
>   that night long past which bred a child for us
>   to send you to your death and leave
>   a mother making children with her son?
>   And then she groaned and cursed the bed in which
>   she brought forth husband by her husband, children
>   by her own child.
>
> (l. 1242ff.)

(speaking of Oedipus):

>   He tore the brooches—
>   the gold chased brooches fastening her robe—
>   away from her and lifting them up high
>   dashed them on his own eyeballs, shrieking out
>   such things as: They will never see the crime
>   I have committed or had done upon me!
>   Dark eyes, now in the days to come look on
>   forbidden faces, do not recognize
>   those whom you long for.
>
> (l. 1268ff.)

Here the action in itself has already become an image, and the diction too: the image depends on the fact that physical and spiritual sight have been combined—it can hardly be the physical sight of Oedipus now that becomes aware of his past actions. "Committed" and "had done upon me" are polar expressions, referring to the whole of existence, and they should not be interpreted as a paraphrase for the marriage unwittingly contracted and his murder of Laius; on the contrary, the phrase signifies that he has "committed" and "had crimes done upon" him in a reversal of the normal sense. In the future "darkness" there will be a "seeing" and a "not seeing," as there has been until now in the light: a seeing of things which he should never have seen with his eyes; and a not seeing, a not knowing of people whom he would wish to see: for thus he was driven by his will to discover his origins; in the "darkness," the physical and spiritual darkness: for it is with this that his real seeing begins, in the form of recognition out of the night of blindness, recognition which is self-recognition. In the same way as Jocasta had left the stage earlier on with a speech in a form resembling a riddle or *griphos* (ll. 1249–50), here, too, the *griphos*-like tangle indicates the tangled nature of Oedipus's fate, in which blindness and seeing are confused.

Finally, the last lament shows again, this time in lyrics, how the particular case contains a more general significance, and how the physical fate contains a spiritual one as well: the "suffering" is "twofold" (l. 1320). In the rather similar lament in the *Ajax,* "'night" and "light" stand for the realms of "life" and "death" which the sufferer transposes as he pours out a torrent of lament invoking both; here in the *Oedipus* the lament goes beyond its literal meaning, so that "darkness" means both physical blindness and the threatening darkness of fate and the daimon:

> AJAX: O
> Darkness that is my light
> Murk of the underworld, my only brightness,
> Oh, take me to yourself to be your dweller.
>
> (l. 394ff.)

By contrast, in the *Oedipus Tyrannus:*

> Darkness!
> Horror of darkness enfolding, resistless, unspeakable visitant
> sped by an ill wind in haste!
> madness and stabbing pain and memory
> of evil deeds I have done!
>
> (l. 1313ff.)

Again, it seems characteristic of the *Ajax* and the *Trachiniae* as opposed to the *Oedipus* that the sinister and threatening region into which the *Oedipus* is continually reaching is not given a name in the two earlier plays, nor does it enter into the situations in them. The Athena who punishes the hero in the *Ajax* is a figure familiar from epic, and as such she takes over and conceals in herself the role of the enigmatic and sinister element, the "cloud" which looms over man's splendour in the *Oedipus,* independent of any character and hardly given a name, not even that of Apollo.

Something which is peculiar to Attic tragedy as a whole, the habit of luxuriating in horror, of investing terror with a kind of voluptuousness, has in this play more than any other extended into the attitude of the tragic hero. Whereas elsewhere the choruses, the words, the poetry, but not the unconscious victims, luxuriated in the delights of pain, here the victim and the one who luxuriates, writhing and pointing to himself, flowering in his torment, speaking and singing out the burden of his obsession, are one and the same. Now there are no biers, no *ekkyklema,* no apparatus: from inside the house the blinded man calls for someone to open the door and lead him to the light. Instead of being brought in, put on show so that men can point him out, the victim is eager to put himself on show, to display the monstrous discovery that he has made in his search for himself: the blinded man that he has been all along. And the traditional action of display, such as the exhibition of the bloodstained Heracles, as he throws back his coverings to show the state that he is in, or of the bloodstained dummy which represents Ajax, sword in breast—for the covers were only thrown over it so that it could be uncovered afterwards (*Ajax*)—this piece of tragic stage action, with its archaic colouring, in the *Oedipus* becomes for the first time part of the figure of the hero himself; whereas the exhibition of the dead Ajax and the dying Heracles remain merely something which is done to them, here the exhibition is a gesture and action of self-exposure, which cannot be divorced from the character of Oedipus himself.

Everything which had surrounded and supported Oedipus, the whole world around him, ancestors and contemporaries, parents and children, city and people, his own rank and his own royal judgment (l. 1369ff.), all these expel him: how is he to "see his children," his "city" with its "towers," its "images of the gods," his people amongst whom he grew up to be regarded as the noblest of all men—expelled as he is from now on both from the realm of the living and from the realm of the dead: even death, as a home-going, as the gathering of a man to his own, would be some sort of belonging; but this, even as a possibility, is totally denied with all the vehemence of tragic unconditionality:

CHORUS: You would be better dead than blind and living.
OEDIPUS: What I have done here was best done—don't tell
me otherwise, do not give me further counsel.

(l. 1368ff.)

It is Ajax in reverse, as it were: no longer a man who calls "death to his aid," who remembers in his last wishes the world of his fate that surrounds him—Zeus and the Erinyes, Salamis and Troy, river and field, Hades and the light—but a man who, if it were only possible, would like nothing better than to destroy his hearing too and thus "dam up" all the "sources" by means of which he participates in the world (l. 1388).

And the apostrophes in the finale, which are usually addressed to friends, intimates and relations—in the *Trachiniae* to the hero's own arms, shoulders and bodily strength, in the *Ajax* to the scene of his heroic deeds, in the *Antigone* to the dead of the family—are now addressed to what had been estranged, inimical, false, from the beginning:

OEDIPUS: Cithaeron, why did you receive me? . . .
O Polybus and Corinth and the house . . .
Crossroads,
and hidden glade . . .
O marriage, marriage!
you bred me and again when you had bred
bred children of your child.

(l. 1391ff.)

Now for the first time the apostrophes become in themselves tragic figures of speech, since they are directed against the very man who utters them—an invocation of the life which is turning against itself. And in the end the revelation, with its last requests, becomes in itself a tragic form, because it is self-contradictory, self-destructive, denying itself through its own actions. Oedipus's retraction of his own words and his curse upon them, his fervent request to the others to cover him, kill him or throw him into the sea, to expel him, to do anything to ensure that he shall never again be seen by a single soul— all this is self-contradictory after he himself had cried out to be led into the light. But at the same time this contradiction is part of the very nature of tragic pathos: for it is characteristic of tragic pathos to exult in itself, and in so doing to affirm what in its suffering it denies.

A counterpoint to Oedipus and the curses he calls down on himself is provided by the entry of a nontragic figure: Creon. That same Creon who, when unjustly accused in the *agon* scene, proved that he was in the right, now decides the fate of the polluted outlaw, with down-to-earth sympathy, not even inhumanely or unfeelingly, nor without first consulting the gods. Thus, as the character with no fate, the character alien to fate, Creon serves as the unchanging standard against which all the changes are measured: it is not so long since Oedipus had heartily despised him, yet now, to the fallen hero in his storm of self-abasement, he is the "best of all" as opposed to the "basest" Oedipus (l. 1433); and when he does not prevent the monstrous blind man from touching his daughters once again he is regarded as granting a great favour. Thus, for all his sympathy, he seems all too cold in comparison with Oedipus, whose full heart pours forth love from his sufferings. As one who is safe from tragedy, in his combined role of companion, opponent and friend, he stands in the same relationship to Oedipus as Odysseus to Ajax. But here again we see how in the *Oedipus* the spirit that moves the play has changed by comparison with the *Ajax*. For not only is there no development in the *Ajax,* there is no reversal in the relationship between the opposing forces either: Odysseus stands in the same relationship to Ajax at the end of the play as he does in the beginning. Yet the figure of Odysseus in the epic cycle would not have been resistant to a change in his attitude towards his mortal enemy during his lifetime and after his death. Thus whereas the *Ajax* is a stationary drama, the *Oedipus Tyrannus* moves and turns. At the same time the opposition of the figures in the *Oedipus* is deepened to the point of impenetrability. There is certainly a difference in greatness, nobility and humanity at the end between Oedipus and Creon, greater than is shown in any other drama; and yet it is no longer possible to reduce the contrast to an easy formula, about characterization, for example, or about morality. Opposed to Ajax and his great, but rigid, heroism, stood the mobility, humanity and insight of Odysseus, and the vengefulness, conceit, envy and pettiness of the figures of Menelaus and Agamemnon. In the *Antigone,* self-sacrifice and youth stood opposed to age and the tyrant's self-assertion—in opposition to Oedipus there stands no more than the merely nontragic.

But in this tragic lesson, this *Ecce,* there is one question that has not been raised—a question which no one since Sophocles, not even Euripides, seems to have been able to avoid as soon as they are confronted with tragedy: where does the guilt lie? Admittedly, Oedipus speaks of himself in words which are used of a criminal who is guilty of another's death. But that does not mean that any question was raised about the guilt (αἰτία). Admittedly, the god is named as the author of the deed, yet this is not so that man may get the better of the god, or of himself in the eyes of god, nor that he may wrestle with god, or destroy himself before god for the sake of his guilt, but only to indicate the correlation between man and god: for the naming of a god is part of the lesson: it is a manifestation of god which coincides with a manifestation of man:

> OEDIPUS: It was Apollo, friends, Apollo,
> that brought this bitter bitterness, my sorrows to
> completion.
> But the hand that struck me
> was none but my own.
>
> (l. 1329ff.)

Nor is the language of sacral law, which is certainly heard here, enough to make any difference to this omission. It is rather that the language of sacral law is used because it is concerned with the same rules and foundations of life which are here in question. But there is no search for where the "guilt" lies in the sense of sacral law either. And even if one were to imagine that a court composed of gods or men had acquitted Oedipus of all guilt, like Orestes in Aeschylus, it would still not help him in the least; for what meaning would such an acquittal have in the face of the contradiction between what he has imagined he is, and what he is? Nor would the opposite verdict of "guilty" add anything to his state. Orestes *can* be acquitted, by himself and by others, but Oedipus *cannot* be released from what he has recognized as the truth about himself. The question of responsibility for what happened, wherever it is raised and in whatever form, whether this responsibility lies with men, with gods or with the laws of nature, and whether the answer is yes or no—this question, without which the greatest tragedies of Euripides and Aeschylus are unthinkable, just does not arise in Sophocles. So there is no decision here about justice and atonement—nothing would be more misguided than to regard Oedipus's blinding as an atonement—or about freedom and necessity. What we have had to consider is illusion and truth as the opposing forces between which man is bound, in which he is entangled, and in whose shackles, as he strives towards the highest he can hope for, he is worn down and destroyed.

Ambiguity and Reversal: On the Enigmatic Structure of Oedipus Rex

J. P. Vernant

In his study of ambiguity in Greek literature written in 1939 W. B. Stanford noted that, from the point of view of ambiguity, *Oedipus Rex* is quite exceptional. This work can be taken as a model. No literary genre of antiquity made such full use of the double entendre as did tragedy and *Oedipus Rex* contains more than twice as many ambiguous expressions as Sophocles' other plays (fifty, according to the count made by Hug in 1872). However, the problem is not so much one of quantity as of nature and function. All the Greek tragedians have recourse to ambiguity as a means of expression and as a modality of thought. But the double meaning takes on a quite different role depending on its place in the organisation of the tragedy and the level of language at which the tragic poet is using it.

It may be a matter of an ambiguity in the vocabulary corresponding to what Aristotle calls *homōnumía* (lexical ambiguity); such an ambiguity is made possible by the shifts or contradictions in the language. The dramatist plays on this to transmit his tragic vision of a world divided against itself and rent with contradictions. On the lips of different characters the same words take on different or opposed meanings because their semantic significance is not the same in religious, legal, political and common parlance. Thus for Antigone, *nómos* denotes the opposite to what Creon, in the particular position in which he is placed, also calls *nómos*. For the girl the word means "religious rule"; for Creon it means "an edict promulgated by the head of state." And, in truth, the semantic field of *nómos* is broad

From *Tragedy and Myth in Ancient Greece.* © 1981 by the Harvester Press Ltd.

enough to cover, among others, both these meanings. In these circumstances the ambiguity conveys the tension between certain meanings felt to be irreconcilable despite their homonymy. Instead of establishing communication and agreement between the characters, the words they exchange on the stage on the contrary underline the impermeability of their minds, the barrier between them. They emphasise the obstacles that separate them and mark out the lines along which conflict will develop. For each hero, enclosed within his own particular world, the word has one and only one meaning. One unilateral position comes into violent conflict with another. The irony of the tragedy may consist in showing how, in the course of the action, the hero finds himself literally "taken at his word," a word which recoils against him, bringing him bitter experience of the meaning he was determined not to recognise. It is only over the heads of the protagonists that, between the author and the spectator, another dialogue is set up in which language regains its ability to establish communication and, as it were, its transparency. But what the tragic message, when understood, conveys is precisely that within the words men exchange there exist areas of opacity and incommunicability. By seeing the protagonists on the stage clinging exclusively to one meaning and thus, in their blindness, bringing about their own destruction or tearing each other to pieces, the spectator is brought to realise that in reality there are two or even more possible meanings. The tragic message becomes intelligible to him to the extent that, abandoning his former certainty and limitations, he becomes aware of the ambiguity of words, of meanings and of the human condition. Recognising that it is the nature of the universe to be in conflict, and accepting a problematical view of the world, the spectator himself, through the spectacle, acquires a tragic consciousness.

Aeschylus's *Agamemnon* provides excellent examples of another type of tragic ambiguity: veiled implications consciously employed by certain characters in the drama who in this way mask within the speech they address to their interlocutor another speech, the opposite of the first, whose meaning is perceptible only to those on the stage and in the audience who possess the necessary information. When greeting Agamemnon on the threshold of the palace, Clytemnestra makes use of this language with a double register. In the ears of the husband it has the pleasant ring of a pledge of love and conjugal fidelity; for the chorus it is already equivocal and they sense some threat within it, while the spectator can see its full sinister quality because he can decode in it the death plot that she has hatched against her husband. Here the ambiguity conveys not a conflict of meanings but the duplicity of a particular character. It is a duplicity of almost demoniacal proportions. The same speech, the very words that draw Agamemnon into the trap, disguising the danger from him, at the same time announce the crime about to be perpetrated to the world in general. And because the queen, in her hatred for her husband, becomes in the course of the drama the instrument of divine justice, the secret speech concealed within her words of welcome takes on an oracular significance. By pronouncing the death of the king she makes it inevitable, like a prophet. So it is in fact the truth that Agamemnon fails to understand in Clytemnestra's words. Once spoken, the speech acquires all the practical force of a curse: what it pronounces it registers in existence, in advance and forever. The ambiguity of the queen's speech is exactly matched by the ambiguity of the symbolical values attached to the purple carpet she has had spread before the king and on which she persuades him to step. When he enters his palace, as Clytemnestra bids him, in terms that at the same time suggest quite another dwelling place, it is indeed the threshold to Hades that Agamemnon, without knowing it, crosses. When he places his bare foot upon the sumptuous cloths with which the ground has been spread, the "purple path" created beneath his steps is not, as he imagines, an almost excessive consecration of his glory but instead a way to deliver him over to the powers of the underworld, to condemn him without remission to death, to the "red" death that comes to him in the same "sumptuous cloths" that Clytemnestra has prepared in advance to trap him, as in a net.

The ambiguity one finds in *Oedipus Rex* is quite different. It is concerned neither with a conflict in meanings nor with the duplicity of the character controlling the action and taking pleasure in playing with his or her victim. In the drama in which he is the victim, it is Oedipus and only Oedipus who pulls the strings. Except for his own obstinate determination to unmask the guilty party, the lofty idea he had of his duty, his capacities, his judgment (his *gnōmē*), and his passionate desire to learn the truth at all costs, there is nothing to oblige him to pursue the enquiry to its end. One after another Tiresias, Jocasta and the shepherd all try to deter him. But in vain. He is not a man to content himself with half-measures or settle for a compromise. Oedipus goes all the way. And at the end of the road that he, despite and against everyone, has followed, he finds that even while it was from start to finish he who pulled the strings it is he who from start to finish has been duped. Thus, at the very moment when he recognises his own responsibility in forging his misfortunes with his own hands, he accuses the gods of having prepared and done it all. The equivocal character of Oedipus's words reflects the ambiguous status that the drama confers upon him and on which the entire tragedy rests. When Oedipus speaks he sometimes says something other than or even the opposite of what he thinks he is saying. The ambiguity of what he says does not reflect a duplicity in his character, which is perfectly consistent, but, more profoundly, the duality of his being. Oedipus is double. He is, in himself, a riddle whose meaning he can only guess when he discovers himself to be in every respect the opposite of what he thought he was and appeared to be. Oedipus himself does not understand the secret speech that, without his realising, lurks at the heart of what he says. And, except for Tiresias, no witness to the drama on stage is capable of perceiving it either. It is the gods who send Oedipus's own speech back at him, deformed or twisted round, like an echo to some of his own words. And this inverted echo, which has the ring of a sinister burst of laughter, in reality sets the record straight. The only authentic truth in Oedipus's words is what he says without meaning to and without understanding it. In this way the twofold dimension of Oedipus's speech is an inverted reflection of the language of the gods as expressed in the enigmatic pronouncement of the oracle. The gods know and speak the truth but they make it manifest by formulating it in words which appear to men to be saying something quite different. Oedipus neither knows nor speaks the truth but the words he uses to say something other than the truth make it startlingly obvious—although Oedipus does not realise this—for whoever has the gift of double hearing in the same way as the diviner has second sight. Oedipus's language thus seems the point at which, within the very same words, two different types of discourse, a human and a divine one, are interwoven and come into conflict. At the beginning they are quite distinct and separate from each other; by the end of the drama, when all is revealed, the human discourse is stood on its head and transformed into its own opposite: the two types of discourse become as one and the riddle is solved. Seated on the stepped slopes of the theater, the spectators occupy a privileged position which enables them, like the gods, to hear and understand the two opposed types of discourse at the same time, following the conflict between them right through from start to finish.

So it is easy to see how it is that, from the point of view of ambiguity, *Oedipus Rex* has the force of a model. Aristotle, noting that the two fundamental elements of a tragic tale, apart from the "pathetic," are recognition (ἀναγνώρισις) and the peripeteia, (περιπέτεια), that is to say the reversal of the action into its contrary (εἰς τὸ ἐναντίον τῶν πραττομένων μεταβολή), points out that in *Oedipus Rex* the recognition is finest because it coincides with the peripeteia. Oedipus's recognition in effect has bearing upon none other than himself. And the hero's final self-identification constitutes a complete reversal of the action in both the senses that can be given to Aristotle's words (words which are themselves not devoid of ambiguity): firstly, Oedipus's situation, from the very fact of recognition, turns out to be the contrary of what it was before; secondly, Oedipus's action ultimately brings about a result that is the opposite of that intended. At the beginning of the drama the stranger from Corinth, the solver of riddles and saviour of Thebes, installed at the head of the city and revered like a god by the people for his knowledge and devotion to public affairs, is confronted with another riddle, the death of the former king. Who killed Laius? At the end of the enquiry the purveyor of justice discovers himself to be also the assassin. Developing behind the gradual unfolding of the detective story that provides the material of the drama is Oedipus's recognition of his own identity. When he appears for the first time at the beginning of the play, telling the suppliants of his determination to discover the criminal at all costs and of his confidence of success, he expresses himself in terms whose ambiguity emphasises the fact that behind the question that he thinks he is answering (who killed Laius?) can be detected the outlines of another problem (who is Oedipus?). The king proudly declares: "By going right back, in my turn, to the beginning (of the events that have remained unknown) I am the one who will bring them to light, ἐγὼ φανῶ." The scholiast does not fail to point out that something lies hidden in the *egò phanô*, something that Oedipus did not mean but that the spectator understands "since everything will be discovered in Oedipus himself, ἐπεὶ τὸ πᾶν ἐν αὐτῷ φανήσεται." *Egò phanô* means "it is I who will bring the criminal to light" but also "I shall discover myself to be the criminal."

What then is Oedipus? Like his own discourse, like the pronouncement of the oracle, Oedipus is double, enigmatic. Psychologically and morally he remains the same from beginning to end in the drama: a man of action and decision, unfailing courage and domineering intelligence who can be accused of no moral fault and no deliberate failing where justice is concerned. But, without his knowing it, without having wished or deserved it, the figure of Oedipus proves to be in every aspect—social, religious and human—the opposite of what, as leader of the city, he seems to be. The Corinthian stranger is in reality a native of Thebes; the solver of riddles is a riddle he himself cannot solve; the dispenser of justice is a criminal; the clairvoyant, a blind man; the saviour of the town, its doom. Oedipus, he who is renowned to all, the first among men, the best of mortals, the man of power, intelligence, honours and wealth discovers himself to be the last, the most unfortunate and the worst of men, a criminal, a defilement, an object of horror to his fellows, abhorred by the gods, reduced to a life of beggary and exile.

Two features emphasise the significance of this "reversal" in Oedipus's condition. In his very first words to him, the priest of Zeus refers to Oedipus as though he were in some way the equal of the gods: ἰσούμενος θεοῖσι. When the riddle is solved the chorus recognises in Oedipus the model of a human life which, through this paradigm, it sees as the equal of nothing at all, ἴσα καὶ τὸ μηδέν. To start with Oedipus is the mind with second sight, the lucid intelligence which, without anybody's aid, helped by neither god nor man, was able, by virtue of his own *gnōmē* alone, to guess the riddle of the Sphinx. He has nothing but scorn for the blind gaze of the diviner whose eyes are closed to the light of the sun and who, in his own words, "lives by the shadows alone." But when the shadows have been dispersed and all has become clear, when light has been shed on Oedipus, precisely then is it that he sees the daylight for the last time. As soon as Oedipus has been "elucidated," uncovered, presented as a spectacle of horror for all to see it is no longer possible for him either to see or to be seen. The Thebans turn their eyes away from him, unable to contemplate full in the face this evil "so frightful to behold," this distress the description and sight of which is too much to bear. And if Oedipus blinds his eyes it is, as he explains, because it has become impossible for him to bear the look of any human creature among either the living or the dead. If it had been possible he would also have stopped up his ears so as to immure himself in a solitude that would cut him off from the society of men.

The light that the gods have cast upon Oedipus is too dazzling for any mortal eye to withstand. It casts Oedipus out of this world that is made for the light of the sun, the human gaze and social contact, and restores him to the solitary world of night in which Tiresias lives: Tiresias with the gift of second sight, who has also paid with his eyes for having acceded to the other light, the blinding, terrible light of the divine.

Seen from a human point of view, Oedipus is the leader with second sight, the equal of the gods; considered from the point of view of the gods he is blind, equal to nothing. Both the reversal of the action and the ambiguity of the language reflect the duality of the human condition which, just like a riddle, lends itself to two opposite interpretations. Human language is reversed when the gods express themselves through it. The human condition is reversed—however great, just and fortunate one may be—as soon as it is scrutinised in relation to the gods. Oedipus had "shot his arrow further than other men, he had won the most fortunate happiness." But in the sight of the Immortals he who rises highest is also the lowest. Oedipus the fortunate reaches the depths of misfortune. As the chorus puts it, "What man has known any but an illusory happiness from which he later falls into disillusion? Taking your destiny as an example, yes yours, unhappy Oedipus, I cannot believe any human life to be a happy one."

If this is indeed the meaning of the tragedy, as Greek scholars believe it to be, it will be recognised that *Oedipus Rex* is not only centered on the theme of the riddle but that in its presentation, development and resolution the play is itself constructed as a riddle. The ambiguity, recognition and peripeteia all parallel one another and are all equally integral to the enigmatical structure of the work. The keystone of the tragic structure, the model that serves as matrix for its dramatic construction and language, is reversal. By this we mean the formal schema in which positive becomes negative when one passes from the one to the other of the two levels, human and divine, that tragedy unites and opposes in the same way as, in Aristotle's definition, riddles join together terms that are irreconcilable.

This logical schema of reversal, corresponding with the ambiguous type of thought that is characteristic of tragedy, offers the spectators a particular kind of lesson: man is not a being that can be described or defined; he is a problem, a riddle the double meanings of which are inexhaustible. The significance of the work is neither psychological nor moral; it is specifically tragic. Parricide and incest do not correspond either with Oedipus's character, his *êthos,* nor with any moral fault, *adikía,* that he has committed. If he kills his father and sleeps with his mother it is not because, in some obscure way, he hates the former and is in love with the latter. Oedipus's feelings for those whom he believes to be his real and only parents, Merope and Polybus, are those of tender filial affection. When he kills Laius it is in legitimate defence against a stranger who struck him first; when he marries Jocasta it is not a love-match but marriage with a stranger which the city of Thebes imposes upon him so that, as reward for his exploit, he can ascend the throne: "The city bound me to a fateful marriage, an accursed union, without my knowing . . . I received this gift that I should never have received from Thebes, after serving her so well." As Oedipus himself declares, in committing parricide and incest neither his person (*sôma*) nor his actions (*érga*) were to blame. In reality he himself has done nothing (οὐκ ἔρξεα). Or rather, while he was committing an action, its meaning became reversed without his knowledge and through no fault of his. Legitimate defence turned into parricide; marriage, the consecration of his honour, turned into incest. Although innocent and pure from the point of view of human law, he is guilty and defiled from the point of view of religion. What he has done without knowing it and with no evil intent or criminal volition is, notwithstanding, the most terrible crime against the sacred order that governs human life. Like birds that eat the flesh of birds, to borrow Aeschylus's expression, he has twice satiated himself with his own flesh, first by shedding the blood of his father and then by becoming united with the blood of his mother. Through a divine curse as gratuitous as the divine choice that singles out other heroes of legend and from which they benefit, Oedipus thus finds himself cut off from society, rejected by humanity. Henceforth he is *ápolis,* the embodiment of the outsider. In his solitude he seems both lower than humanity—a wild beast or savage monster—and higher than it, stamped as he is, like a *daímōn,* with a religious quality to be feared. His defilement, his *ágos* is simply the reverse side to the supernatural power that has concentrated itself in him to bring him to his doom: defiled as he is, he is also consecrated and holy, he is *hierós* and *eusebếs.* To the city that takes him in and to the land that receives his corpse he guarantees the greatest of blessings.

This network of reversals makes its impact through stylistic and dramatic devices as well as through ambiguous expressions—in particular through what Bernard Knox calls an inversion in the use of the same terms in the course of the tragic action. We can only refer the reader here to his fine study from which we will take no more than a few examples. One way of effecting this reversal is by describing Oedipus's condition in terms whose meanings are systematically inverted as one passes from an active to a passive construction. Oedipus is described as a hunter on the trail, tracking down and flushing out the wild beast at large in the mountains, pursuing and putting it to flight, relegating it to a place far from human beings. But in this hunt the hunter ultimately finds himself the quarry: pursued by the terrible curse of his parents, Oedipus wanders away, howling like a wild animal, before putting out his eyes and fleeing into the wild mountains of Cithaeron. Oedipus heads an investigation which is both legal and scientific, as is stressed by the repeated use of the verb *zēteîn*. But the investigator is also the object of the investigation, the *zētôn* is also the *zētoúmenon* just as the examiner or questioner is also the answer to the question. Oedipus is both the one who discovers and the object of the discovery, the very one who is discovered. He is the doctor who speaks of the evil from which the city is suffering in medical terms, but he is also the one who is diseased and the disease itself.

Another form of reversal is the following: the terms used to describe Oedipus at the height of his glory one by one become detached from him and applied instead to the figures of the gods. The greatness of Oedipus shrinks to nothing as the greatness of the gods, in contrast with his, becomes increasingly evident. In line 14 the priest of Zeus with his first words addresses Oedipus as sovereign: *kratúnōn;* in line 903 the chorus prays to Zeus as sovereign: *ô kratúnōn*. In line 48 the Thebans call Oedipus their saviour: *sōtḗr;* in line 150 it is Apollo who is invoked as saviour, to put an end (*paustḗrios*) to the evil, as Oedipus earlier "put an end" to the Sphinx. At 237 Oedipus gives orders in his capacity as master of power and of the throne (ἐγὼ κράτη τε καὶ θρόνους νέμω); at 201 the chorus prays to Zeus as "master of power and of the thunderbolt" (ἀστραπᾶν κράτη νέμων). At 441, Oedipus recalls the exploit that made him great (*mégas*); at 871, the chorus recalls that amid the heavenly laws there lives a great (*mégas*) god who never ages. The dominion (*archḗ*) that Oedipus flatters himself he wields is recognised by the chorus to lie, forever immortal, between the hands of Zeus. The help (*alkḗ*) that the priest begs from Oedipus at line 42 is sought by the chorus from Athena at 189. In the first line of the tragedy Oedipus addresses the suppliants as a father his children; but at 202 the chorus gives the title of father to Zeus, imploring him to rid the city of its pestilence: *ô̂ Zeû páter*.

The very name of Oedipus lends itself to such effects of reversal. He himself is ambiguous, stamped with the enigmatic character that is the mark of the entire tragedy. Oedipus is the man with the swollen foot (*oîdos*), an infirmity that recalls the accursed child rejected by its parents and exposed to savage nature to die. But Oedipus is also the man who knows (*oîda*) the riddle of the foot and who succeeds in deciphering, without twisting its meaning, the oracle of the Sphinx, the sinister prophetess, her of the obscure song. This is the knowledge that sets the foreign hero on the throne of Thebes in the place of its legitimate heirs. The double meaning of Oedipus is to be found in the name itself in the opposition between the first two syllables and the third. *Oîda;* I know: this is one of the key words on the lips of Oedipus triumphant, of Oedipus the tyrant. *Poús:* foot: the mark stamped at birth on one whose destiny is to end up as he began, as one excluded like the wild beast whose foot makes it flee, whose foot isolates him from other men, who hopes in vain to escape the oracles, pursued by the curse of the terrible foot for having infringed the sacred laws with a foot raised high and unable henceforth to free his foot from the misfortunes into which he has cast himself by raising himself to the highest position of power. The whole of the tragedy of Oedipus seems to be contained in the play to which the riddle of his name lends itself. The eminently knowledgeable master of Thebes, protected by Good Luck, seems to be opposed on every point by the accursed child, the *Swollen Foot* rejected by his native land. But before Oedipus can know who he really is, the first of his two personalities, the one he first assumes, must be so thoroughly inverted that it becomes as one with the second.

When Oedipus solves the Sphinx's riddle the solution his wisdom discovers is, in a way, already relevant to himself. The baleful songstress' question is: who is the being that is at the same time *dípous, trípous,* and *tetrápous?* For *oi-dípous* the mystery is an apparent, not a real one: of course the answer is himself, man. But his reply is only apparent, not real knowledge: the true problem that is still masked is: what then is man, what is Oedipus? Oedipus's pseudo-reply makes Thebes open wide her gates to him. But by installing him at the head of the State, it is also the instrument that, while misleading him as to his true identity, brings about his parricide and incest. For Oedipus, resolving his own mystery involves recognising in the stranger who is the ruler of Thebes the child who was native to that country and formerly rejected by it. However, this identification does not integrate Oedipus definitively into the country that is his own and establish him on the throne he occupies as the legitimate son of the king rather than as a foreign tyrant. Instead, it turns him into a monster that must be expelled forever from the town and cut off from the world of human beings.

The figure of Oedipus the Sage, placed far above other men, is revered like a god as the unchallenged master of justice who holds in his hands the salvation of the entire city. But at the end of the drama this figure is inverted into its opposite; reduced to the lowest degree of degradation, we find Oedipus-the-Swollen-Foot, the abominable defilement in whom all the world's impurity is concentrated. The divine king, the purifier and saviour of his people becomes one with the defiled criminal who must be expelled like a *pharmakós* or scapegoat so that the town can regain its purity and be saved.

It is this axis on which the divine king occupies the highest point and the *pharmakós* the lowest that governs the whole series of reversals that affect the figure of Oedipus and turn the hero into a "paradigm" of ambiguous, tragic man.

The quasi-divine character of the majestic figure advancing to the threshold of his palace at the beginning of the tragedy has not failed to strike the commentators. Even the ancient scholiast noted, in his commentary to line 16, that the suppliants approach the altars of the royal house as if these were the altars of some god. The expression used by Zeus's priest: "You behold us assembled close to *your* altars" seems all the more loaded with significance in that Oedipus himself asks: "Why do you thus kneel in a posture of ritual supplication before me, with your wreaths crowned with bands?" This veneration for a man who is placed higher than other men because he has saved the town "with the help of a god," because he has, by some supernatural favour, revealed himself to be *Túchē,* the city's Good Luck, persists unabated from beginning to end of the play. Even after the revelation of Oedipus's double defilement the chorus still praises as its saviour the one whom it calls "my king" who "stood like a tower in the face of death." Even as it describes the unexpiatable crimes of the unfortunate Oedipus, the chorus concludes by saying: "And yet, to tell the truth, it is thanks to you that I have been able to draw breath again and find rest."

But it is at the most crucial point in the drama, when the fate of Oedipus rests on a razor's edge, that the polarity between the status of demigod and that of scapegoat is the most clearly apparent. The situation at this point is as follows: it is already known that Oedipus may be the murderer of Laius; the agreement in the oracles pronounced on the one hand to Oedipus and on the other to Laius and Jocasta increases the dread that oppresses the hearts of the protagonists and Theban notables. Then the messenger from Corinth arrives; he announces that Oedipus is not the son of those whom he believes to be his parents; he is a foundling; the messenger himself received him from the hands of a shepherd on Mount Cithaeron. Jocasta, for whom everything has now become clear, entreats Oedipus not to pursue the enquiry any further. Oedipus refuses. The queen then warns him for the last time: "Wretch, may you never know who you are!" But yet again the tyrant of Thebes misunderstands the meaning of what it is to be Oedipus. He thinks that the queen is afraid to hear that the foundling's birth was a lowly one and that her marriage turns out to be a misalliance with a nobody, a slave, a son of slaves to the third generation. It is precisely at this point that Oedipus finds new heart. The messenger's account arouses in his dejected spirits the wild hope that the chorus shares with him and proceeds to express with joy. Oedipus declares himself to be the son of *Túchē,* Good Luck, who in the course of the years has reversed the situation, changing him from "small" to "great," who, in other words, has transformed the misshapen foundling into the wise master of Thebes. The words are full of irony: Oedipus is no son of *Túchē* but, as Tiresias predicted, her victim; and the "reversal" is the opposite one, reducing the great Oedipus to the smallest stature possible, bringing the equal of the gods down to the equal of nothing at all.

Yet the false impression that Oedipus and the chorus share is an understandable one. The exposed child may be a reject to be got rid of, a misshapen monster or a humble slave. But he may also be a hero with an exceptional destiny. Saved from death and victor in the trial imposed upon him at his birth, the exile reveals himself to be a chosen one invested with supernatural powers. Now that he has returned in triumph to the country that expelled him, he will live there not as an ordinary citizen but as its absolute master, reigning over his subjects like a god set down in the midst of men. This is why the theme of the exposed child appears in almost all of the Greek legends about heroes. If Oedipus was at birth rejected in this way, cut off from his human lineage, it is no doubt—the chorus imagines—because he is the son of some god, of the nymphs of Cithaeron, of Pan or of Apollo, Hermes or Dionysus.

This mythical image of the hero exposed and saved, rejected and returning in triumph, is continued in the fifth century in a transposed form, in one particular representation of the *túrannos*. Like the hero, the tyrant accedes to royalty via an indirect route, bypassing the legitimate line; like him, his qualifications for power are his actions and his exploits. He reigns by virtue not of his blood but of his own qualities; he is the son of his works and also of Good Luck. The supreme power that he has succeeded in winning outside the ordinary norms places him, for better or worse, above other men and above the law. As B. Knox rightly observes, the comparison of tyranny to the power of the gods—and the Greeks defined these as "the most strong," "the most powerful"—is a commonplace in the literature of the fifth and fourth centuries. Euripides and Plato both speak of the τυραννὶς ἰσόθεος, tyranny that is the equal of a god in that it is the absolute power to do as one wishes, to do anything one wants.

The other, complementary and opposed side of Oedipus, his role as a scapegoat, has not been so clearly noted by the commentators. It was certainly noticed that, at the end of the tragedy, Oedipus is hounded from Thebes just as the *homo piacularis* is expelled so as to "remove the defilement," τὸ ἄγος ἐλαύνειν. But it was Louis Gernet who first made a precise link between the theme of the tragedy and the Athenian ritual of the *pharmakós*.

Thebes suffers from a *loimós* which manifests itself, in the traditional way, by the failure of all sources of fertility: earth, flocks and women are no longer productive while at the same time plague decimates the living. Sterility, disease and death are all felt to be the power of the same defilement, a *míasma* that has disrupted the whole of life's normal course. What must be done is find the criminal who is the city's defilement or *ágos,* and eliminate the ill by eliminating him. As is well known, this is what was done at Athens, in the seventh century, to expiate the impious murder of Kylon, when the

Alcmeonids were declared impure and sacrilegious and expelled, ἐναγεῖς καὶ ἀλιτήριοι.

But in Athens, as in other Greek cities, there was also an annual ritual aimed at the periodical expulsion of all the defilement accumulated over the past year. Helladius of Byzantium reports as follows: "It is the custom in Athens to parade two *pharmakoí,* with the object of purification, one for the men, the other for the women"! According to legend the origin of the ritual was the Athenians' impious murder of Androgaeus the Cretan. To remove the *loimós* released by the crime, the custom of repeated purification by means of *pharmakói* was introduced. The ceremony took place on the first day of the festival of the Thargelia, on the sixth day of the month of *Thargeliōn.* The two *pharmakoí,* wearing necklaces of dried figs (black or green, according to which sex they represented), were paraded through the town; they were beaten about their sexual organs with scilla bulbs, figs and other wild plants, and then expelled. In the earliest days at least, they were possibly stoned to death, their corpses burnt and their ashes strewn to the winds. How were these *pharmakoí* selected? They were most likely recruited from the dregs of the population, from among the *kakoûrgoi,* gibbet fodder whose crimes, physical ugliness, lowly condition and base and repugnant occupations marked them out as inferior, degraded beings, *phaûloi,* the refuse of society. In the *Frogs,* Aristophanes contrasts the well-born citizens who are wise, just, good and honest, resembling the sound city currency, with the false coins of copper, "the foreigners, rascals, knaves, sons of knaves, and newcomers whom the city would not easily have chosen at random, even for *pharmakoí.* Tzetzes, citing fragments from the poet Hipponax, notes that when a *loimós* afflicted the city, they chose the most ugly person of all (*amorphóteron*) as the *katharmós* and *pharmakós* of the stricken town. At Leukas, a criminal under sentence of death was used for the purification. At Marseilles, some poor wretch came forward, offering himself for the salvation of all. He won a year's grace during which he was supported at the expense of the public. When the year had elapsed he was paraded round the town and solemnly cursed so that all the faults of the community should fall upon his head. So it was quite natural that the image of the *pharmakós* should come to Lysias's mind when he was denouncing to the judges the repugnant villainy of a character such as Andocides, impious, sacrilegious, a denunciator and traitor, hounded from one town to another and, in his misfortunes, seemingly marked by the finger of god. To condemn Andocides "is to purify the town, to free it from defilement, to expel the *pharmakós.*"

There was another aspect to the Athenian Thargelia. They combined with the expulsion of the *pharmakós* another ritual which took place on the seventh of the month, the day dedicated to Apollo. The first fruits of the land were consecrated to the god in the form of the *thárgēlos,* a pastry and a pot containing seeds of all kinds. But the central feature of the festival consisted in parading the *eiresiṓné,* an olive or laurel branch garlanded with wool and decorated with fruits, cakes and little phials of oil and wine. Young boys carried these "May trees" through the town, depositing some at the threshold of the temple of Apollo and hanging others outside the doors of private dwellings, πρὸς ἀποτροπὴν λιμοῦ, to ward off famine. The *eiresiṓné* in Attica, Samos, Delos and Rhodes and the *kōpṓ* in Thebes represented the rebirth of springtime. To the accompaniment of songs and a collection of gifts, these processions consecrated the end of the old season and ushered in the young new year under the sign of donations, abundance and health. The Athenian ritual clearly indicates the need for the social group to reinvigorate the forces of fertility on which its life depends, by dismissing those that have, as it were, withered away during the year. The *eiresiṓné* remained hanging outside the doors of the houses, fading and withering, until it was replaced on this day of the Thargelia by another that the new year had made to flourish.

But this renewal symbolised by the *eiresiṓné* could only take place if every defilement had been banished from the group and from the land and men made pure once again. As Plutarch notes, the first fruits of all kinds that adorn the *eiresiṓné* commemorate the end of the *aphoría,* the sterility that afflicted the land of Attica in punishment for the murder of Androgaeus, the very murder that the expulsion of the *pharmakós* is intended to expiate. The major role played by the *eiresiṓné* in the Thargelia explains why Hesychius glosses Θάργηλος by ἡἱκετηρία, for in form and in function the *eiresiṓné* is exactly like the branch carried by a suppliant.

These *hiketeríai,* these suppliants' branches festooned with wool, are precisely what, at the beginning of Sophocles' drama, the representatives of Theban youth, children and very young people divided into age groups, carry in procession to the doors of the royal palace and deposit before the altars of Apollo to conjure away the *loimós* that afflicts the town. Another detail makes it possible to define more

precisely the ritual procedure depicted in the first scene of the tragedy. We are twice told that the town is loud with "paeons mingled
with tears and lamentation." Normally the paeon is a joyful song for
victory and for actions of magnanimity. It stands in contrast to the
threnody: the chant of mourning or plaintive dirge. But we know
through a scholiast to the *Iliad* that there is also another kind of paeon
that is "sung to bring about the end of evils or to avert them."
According to the scholiast, this cathartic paeon, the memory of which
was perpetuated in particular by the Pythagoreans, might equally
well appear as a threnody. This is the paeon mingled with sobs
mentioned in the tragedy. This purificatory song is sung at a very
precise moment in the religious calendar, at the turning point of the
year represented by the season of spring which, at the threshold of
summer, marks the start of the period of human activities that in-
clude harvesting, navigation and warfare. The Thargelia, which take
place in May, before the start of the harvesting, belong to this complex of spring rituals.

These details must have driven home the connection with the
Athenian ritual all the more forcefully to the spectators of the tragedy
given that Oedipus is explicitly presented as the *ágos,* the defilement
that must be expelled. In his very first words he describes himself,
without meaning to, in terms which evoke the figure of the scapegoat: addressing the suppliants, he says "I know very well that you
are all suffering; and as you thus suffer, there is not one of you who
suffers as much as I. For your pain only affects each one of you as an
individual and nobody else, but my soul (*psuchē*) laments over the
town, myself and you, all at once." And a little further on he says,
"I suffer the misfortune of all these men even more than if it were my
own." Oedipus is mistaken; this evil that Creon immediately calls by
its correct name, *míasma, is* in fact his own. But even while under this
misapprehension, he speaks truly without realising it: it is because, as
the *míasma,* he is himself the *ágos* of the city that Oedipus does indeed
carry the whole weight of all the misfortune that afflicts his fellow-
citizens.

Divine king and *pharmakós:* these are the two sides to Oedipus
that make a riddle of him by combining within him two figures, the
one the reverse of the other, as in a formula with a double meaning.
Sophocles lends general significance to this inversion in Oedipus's
nature by presenting the hero as a model of the human condition.
But the polarity between king and scapegoat (a polarity that the

tragedy situates at the very heart of the figure of Oedipus) is something that Sophocles did not need to invent. It was already part of the religious practice and social thought of the Greeks. The poet simply gave it new significance by having it symbolise man and his fundamental ambiguity. If Sophocles chooses the pair *túrannos-pharmakós* to illustrate what we have called the theme of reversal, it is because the two figures appear symmetrical and in some respects interchangeable in their opposition. Both are presented as *individuals* responsible for the *collective* salvation of the group. In Homer and Hesiod the fertility of the land, herds and women depends upon the person of the king, the descendant of Zeus. If he shows himself to be *amumōn*, beyond reproach, in his justice as monarch, then everything in his city prospers; but if he goes astray *the entire town* pays for the fault of *the one individual*. The son of Cronos brings down misfortune, *limós* and *loimós,* both famine and pestilence, upon the whole community. Men die, women no longer bring forth children, the land remains sterile and the herds do not reproduce. So when a divine scourge afflicts a people the normal solution is to sacrifice the king. If he is the master of fertility and this fails it is because his power as sovereign has somehow been turned upside down; his justice has become criminal, his virtue a defilement, the best man (*áristos*) has become the worst (*kákistos*). Thus the legends of Lycurgus, Athamas and Oinoclos involve getting rid of the *loimós* by stoning the king, by his ritual killing or, failing this, his son is sacrificed. But it may also happen that a member of the community is delegated to assume the role of the unworthy sovereign, the role of the king turned inside out. The king unburdens his responsibilities upon an individual who is a kind of inverted image of all that is negative in his own character. This is indeed what the *pharmakós* is; the king's double, but reversed like the carnival kings crowned for the duration of the festival, when order is turned upside down and the social hierarchies reversed: sexual taboos are lifted, theft becomes lawful, slaves take the place of their masters, women exchange their clothes with men—and in these circumstances the one who sits upon the throne must be the lowest, the most ugly, the most ridiculous, the most criminal. But when the festival is over the counterking is expelled or put to death, carrying away with him all the disorder that he embodied and from which he thereby purges the community.

In the ritual of the Thargelia, in classical Athens, certain features that evoke the sovereign, the master of fertility are still detectable in the figure of the *pharmakós*. The revolting figure who has to embody the defilement lives at the expense of the state, feeding on dishes of exceptional purity: fruit, cheese and sacred cakes of *mâza;* he is adorned in the procession, like the *eiresiōnē*, with necklaces of figs and with branches and he is beaten on his sexual organs with scilla bulbs; and the reason for this is that he possesses the beneficent virtue of fertility. His defilement is a religious qualification which can be used to good effect. His *ágos,* like that of Oedipus, turns him into a *katharmós,* a *kathársios,* a purifier. Furthermore, the ambiguity of this figure even comes through in the etiological accounts that are supposed to explain the origins of the ritual. The version of Helladius of Byzantium that we have cited is contradicted by that given by Diogenes Laertius and Athenaeus which runs as follows: when Epimenides was purifying Athens from the *loimós* caused by the murder of Kylon, two young men, one of whom was called Cratinos, voluntarily offered themselves to purify the land that had nourished them. These two young men are presented not as the rejects of society but as the very flower of Athenian youth. According to Tzetzes, as we have seen, a particularly ugly person (ἀμορφότερος) was chosen to be *pharmakós:* according to Athenaeus, Cratinos was on the contrary μειράκιον εὔμορφον, an exceptionally handsome lad.

This symmetry between the *pharmakós* and the king of legend in which the former, at the bottom of the scale, took on a role analogous to that which the latter played at the top, may throw some light upon the institution of ostracism whose many bizarre features have been noted by J. Carcopino. As we know, there is no longer a place within the framework of the city for the figure of the king, the master of fertility. When ostracism became an institution in Athens at the end of the sixth century it was the figure of the tyrant that took over, in a transposed form, certain religious characteristics of the ancient sovereign. The main purpose of ostracism was to remove any citizen who, by rising too high, might accede to the tyranny. But in this positivist form the explanation fails to account for certain archaic features of the institution. It came into operation every year, probably between the sixth and the eighth prytanies, in accordance with rules quite unlike those that governed the ordinary procedures of law and political life. Ostracism was a sentence aimed at "removing a citizen from the city" by imposing a temporary exile lasting ten years. It was not passed by the tribunals but by the assembly, without anybody having been publicly denounced or even accused. At a preliminary hearing it was decided, by a show of hands, whether or not there was any occasion to use the procedure of ostracism that year. No name was mentioned and no debate took place. If the vote was positive the assembly regathered at a meeting called specially, some time later. It was held in the agora not, as was usual, on the Pnyx. The vote itself was taken by each participant writing the name of his choice on a potsherd. Again no debate took place; no name was proposed; there was no accusation and no defence. The vote was passed without any appeal being made to reasons of a political or legal nature. It was all organised so as to make it possible for the popular feeling that the Greeks called *phthónos* (a mixture of envy and religious distrust of anyone who rose too high or was too successful) to manifest itself in the most spontaneous and unanimous fashion (there had to be at least six thousand voters) regardless of any rule of law or rational justification. The only things held against the ostracised man were the very superior qualities which had raised him above the common herd, and his exaggerated good luck which might call down the wrath of the gods upon the town. The fear of tyranny was confused with a more deep-seated religious apprehension directed against one who put the entire group in peril. As Solon wrote, "a city can perish from its too great men, ἀνδρῶν δ'ἐκ μεγάλων πόλις ὄλλυται."

Aristotle's development of the idea of ostracism is characteristic in this respect. He says that if a man oversteps the common level in virtue and in political skill, he cannot be accepted on an equal footing with the rest of the citizens: "Such a being will in effect naturally be as a god among men." And Aristotle goes on to say that this is why the democratic states introduced the institution of ostracism. In doing so they were following the example of myth: the Argonauts abandoned Heracles for a similar reason. The ship Argo refused to carry him like the other passengers, on account of his excessive weight. Aristotle concludes by remarking that the situation is similar in the arts and sciences: "a choir master would not accept among his singers anyone with a voice whose beauty would surpass the whole of the rest of the chorus put together."

How could the city possibly take to its bosom one who, like Oedipus, "has shot his arrow further than anyone else" and has become *isótheos?* In ostracism it creates an institution whose role is symmetrical to and the reverse of the ritual of the Thargelia. In the person of the ostracised one the city expels whatever it is in it that is too high and that embodies the evil that can fall on it from above. In that of the *pharmakós,* it expels whatever is most vile and embodies the evil that threatens it from below. Through this double and complementary rejection it sets its own limits in relation to what is above and what is below. It takes the true measure of man as opposed on the one hand to the divine and the heroic and, on the other, to the bestial and the monstrous.

In his political theory, Aristotle gives explicit and deliberate expression to what the city thus spontaneously brings about through the interplay of its institutions. He declares that man is by nature a political animal; so whoever is found to be by nature *ápolis* is either *phaûlos,* a degraded being, less than a man or else κρείττων ἢ ἄνθρωπος, above humanity, more powerful than man. He goes on to say that such a man is "like an isolated piece at draughts" (ἅτε περ ἄζυξ ὢν ὥσπερ ἐν πεττοῖς) and a little later he returns to this idea when he notes that whoever cannot live in the community "forms no part of the state and so is either a brutish beast or a god (ἢ θηρίον ἢ θεός)."

This is an exact definition of the double and contradictory nature of Oedipus's status; he is above and also below human beings, a hero more powerful than man, the equal of the gods, and at the same time a brutish beast spurned and relegated to the wild solitude of the mountains.

But Aristotle's remark goes even further. It allows us to understand the role of the parricide and perpetrator of incest through the reversal that combines within Oedipus's person one who is both the equal of the gods and the equal of nothing at all. These two crimes in effect constitute an infringement of the basic rules of a game of draughts in which each piece occupies in relation to the others a precise place on the checkerboard of the city. By being guilty of these crimes Oedipus has shuffled the cards, mixed up the positions and pieces: he is now disqualified. Through his parricide followed by incest he instals himself in the place formerly occupied by his father; he makes Jocasta assume the roles of both mother and wife; he identifies himself both with Laius (as the husband of Jocasta) and with his own children (to whom he is both father and brother) and in this way he mixes up the three generations of the lineage. Sophocles underlines this confusion, this identification of what ought to remain distinct and separate, with an emphasis which has sometimes shocked modern readers but which the interpreter must take into full account. He does so by means of a play on words centered on *homós* and *ísos,* similar and equal, together with their compound forms. Even before he knows anything of his true origins Oedipus describes himself, from the point of view of his relationship to Laius, as sharing the same bed and having a *homósporon* wife. On his lips the word means that he is impregnating with his seed the same woman that Laius has impregnated before him; but in line 460 Tiresias gives the word its true meaning: he tells Oedipus that he will discover himself to be both the murderer of his father and his *homósporos,* his co-impregnator. *Homósporos* usually has a different meaning, namely: born of the same seed, blood relative. And indeed, without knowing it, Oedipus is of the same blood as both Laius and Jocasta. The fact that Oedipus and his own sons are equal is expressed in a series of brutally forceful images: the father has sowed the seed for his sons in the very spot where he himself was sown; Jocasta is a wife, is not a wife but a mother whose furrow has produced in a double harvest both the father and the children; Oedipus has sown his seed in the woman who gave him birth, in whom he himself was seeded and from these same furrows, the "equal" furrows, he has obtained his own children. But it is Tiresias who lends the full weight to this terminology expressing equality when he addresses Oedipus as follows: misfortunes will come which "will make you the equal of yourself by making you the equal of your children." The identification of Oedipus with his own father and his own children, the assimilation of mother and wife in the person of Jocasta make Oedipus the equal of himself, that is turn him into an *ágos,* an *ápolis* being incommensurable and without equality with other men, who believing himself to be the equal of a god in the end finds himself to be the equal of nothing at all. For no more than does the wild beast, does the *isótheos* tyrant recognise the rules of the game on which the human city is based. Among the gods, who make up a single family, incest is not forbidden. Kronos and Zeus each attacked and dethroned their own father. Like them, the tyrant may believe that all is permitted to him; Plato calls him a "parricide" and compares him to a man who, by virtue of a magic ring, is free to infringe the most sacred of laws with impunity: he may kill whomever he pleases, be united with whomever he likes; he is "the master who may do anything, like a god among men." Similarly, wild beasts are not obliged, either, to respect the prohibitions upon which human society rests. They are not, as the gods are, above the laws of virtue of their greater powers, but below them through default of *lógos*. Dio Chrysostomus records Diogenes' ironic remark on the subject of Oedipus: "Oedipus bewails the fact that he is both father and brother to his children and husband and son to his wife; but that is something that neither cocks nor dogs nor birds complain about"; for among these creatures there are no such things as brothers, fathers, husbands, sons or wives. Like isolated pieces in a game of draughts, they live without rules, knowing neither difference nor equality, in the confusion of *anomía*.

Disqualified from the game, excluded from the city and rejected by the human race because of his parricide and incest, Oedipus is discovered, at the end of the tragedy, to be identical to the monstrous creature referred to in the riddle which he, in his pride of "wise man" believed he had solved. The Sphinx's question was: what is the creature with one voice which has two, three and four legs? Confusing and mixing them up, it referred to the three successive ages of man that he can only know one after another: he is a child when he crawls on four legs, an adult when he stands firmly on his two feet and an old man leaning on his stick. By identifying himself simultaneously with his young children and his old father, Oedipus, the man standing on his two feet, obliterates the barriers that ought to keep the father strictly separate from the sons and the grandfather so that each human generation occupies its appointed place both in the sequence of time and in the order of the city. Here is the last tragic reversal: it is his victory over the Sphinx that turns Oedipus into, not the solution that he guessed, but the very question posed, not a man like other men but a creature of confusion and chaos, the only creature (we are told) of all those that live upon earth, in the air or in the water who has "changed his nature" instead of keeping it clear and distinct. As formulated by the Sphinx then, the riddle of man does have a solution but it is one that recoils against the monster's victor, the solver of riddles, and reveals him to be himself a kind of monster, a man in the shape of a riddle—and this time a riddle to which there is no solution.

A number of conclusions may be drawn from our analysis of *Oedipus Rex*. Firstly there is one model that is at work in the tragedy on every level at which it operates: in the language, in a number of stylistic features; in the structure of the drama where recognition and *peripeteia* coincide; in the theme of the destiny of Oedipus; and in the person of the hero himself. The model is not set out anywhere as a particular image, idea or complex of feelings. It takes the form of a purely operational schema of reversal, a rule of ambiguous logic. But the tragedy gives content to this form. For instance, in the case of the face presented by Oedipus, the paradigm of the double man, the reversed man, the rule is embodied in the reversal that transforms the divine king into the scapegoat.

Secondly, if the complementary opposition between the *túrannos* and the *pharmakós* on which Sophocles plays is indeed, as we believe, present in the institutions and political theory of the ancient Greeks, is the tragedy doing any more than simply reflecting a structure that already exists in the society and thought of the community? Our own belief is, on the contrary, that far from reflecting this it challenges it, brings it into question. For in social practice and theory, the polar structure of the superhuman and the subhuman is aimed at giving a more precise picture of the specific features of the field of human life as defined by the body of *nómoi* that characterise it. The relationship between the above and the below is merely that between the two lines which clearly define the boundaries within which man is contained. In contrast, in Sophocles, the superhuman and the subhuman meet and become confused within the same figure. And, given that this figure is the model of man, the boundaries that contained human life and made it possible to establish its status without ambiguity are obliterated. When man decides, like Oedipus, to carry the enquiry into what he is as far as it can go, he discovers himself to be enigmatic, without consistency, without any domain of his own or any fixed point of attachment, with no defined essence, oscillating between being the equal of the gods and the equal of nothing at all. His real greatness consists in the very thing that expresses his enigmatic nature: his questioning.

And finally, perhaps the most difficult thing is not, as we have attempted, restoring to tragedy its true meaning, the meaning it had for the Greeks of the fifth century, but rather understanding the misunderstandings that it has given rise to or rather how it is that it has given rise to so many. What is the source of the work of art's relative malleability which accounts for both its fresh and its perennial qualities? If in the last analysis the true mainspring of the tragedy is this kind of reversal that operates as a logical schema, it is understandable that the drama remains open to a number of different interpretations. We can also understand how it is that *Oedipus Rex* has acquired new meanings as, in the course of the history of western thought, the problem of the ambiguity of man has shifted and changed its ground while the enigma of human existence has come to be formulated in different terms from those used by the ancient Greek tragedians.

The Music of the Sphinx: The Problem of Language in *Oedipus Tyrannus*

Charles Segal

No play is more about language than the *Oedipus Tyrannus*. An expert at decoding difficult messages, the hero cannot decode the meaning of his own name. Human communication here parallels the communication by ritual and oracle between man and God. Continually breaking down, this communication either ceases prematurely because of fears or knowledge that cannot be spoken or runs to excess because of passion and anger. Apollo's oracles from above and the Sphinx's riddle from below provide models for human discourse, but both also short-circuit the significative function of language. The oracles are either too terrifyingly specific to be understood, or else conceal beneath apparent generality their specific purport for Oedipus's life ("Drive out the pollution nurtured in the land," l. 97). The riddle, with its plural meanings for each signifier, undermines the denotative and differentiating function of language. It misuses, or perhaps overuses, language, by exploiting its ambiguity rather than its precision. It thereby projects a world whose meaning corresponds to the shifting, uncertain, "enigmatic" quality of language rather than to the potential clarity, definiteness, intelligibility of language.

The play correlates personal identity, language, and the world order as multiple reflections of the hero's failure to find the mediating, ordering terms of civilized life. The oracle veers between images of the world order as chaotic and as deterministic; the riddle-prophecies veer between the undifferentiated and the overspecific;

From *Contemporary Literary Hermeneutics and Interpretations of Classic Texts*, edited by Stephen Kresic. © 1981 by the University of Ottawa Press.

and Oedipus, guided by both oracle and riddle, moves back to the origins of his name.

The very name of the hero links together the search for personal identity and the exploration of the limits of language as a means of interpreting the meaning or meaninglessness of life in a mysterious world. Name and oracle are analogous aspects of the ambiguities of language in its imperfect reflection of reality. In this play the archaeology of knowledge, in Foucault's sense, and the archaeology of the self coincide. Oedipus's search for himself and his origins is also a search for the origin and meaning of his name.

The play begins with Oedipus consulting the oracle on behalf of the whole city. As the action progresses, it takes us back to his lonely and private consultation of the oracle, on his own behalf, after the insult about his legitimate birth—and therefore about his name—at Corinth. The solitary consultation of the now exiled Oedipus (ll. 794–96; cf. l. 787) contrasts also with the escorted visit of Laius. Soon the solitariness of that journey to Delphi becomes the crucial point in Oedipus's relation to his present city; if "one lone-girt man" met Laius in that fatal encounter at the triple roads leading from Delphi to Thebes and Corinth, Oedipus is the murderer (ll. 846–47). The prophecies to both Laius and Oedipus lead also to the wild realm outside the city: Laius exposes a son on a wild mountainside (l. 711ff.); Oedipus leaves the shelter of Corinth for the place where the two oracles join, the desolate crossroads (l. 787ff.)

There are three oracles in the play: one to Thebes in the present, one to Oedipus in the past, and one to Laius in the still remoter past. They come together, ironically, at the point when Jocasta, seeking to disprove the power of oracles (ll. 709–10, 723–25), inadvertently gives Oedipus the clue which proves their accuracy. Her crucial sentence about the triple roads begins, "Robbers killed him, as is the rumor" (ll. 175–76). But that last clause, "as is the rumor," ὥσπερ γ' ἡ φάτις, can also mean, "as (says) the oracle," for the word *phatis* means not only "rumor," but also "prophecy," "oracle," and in fact has that latter meaning in four of its five other occurrences in the play (ll. 151, 310, 323, 1440; cf. l. 495). Even in asserting the falsehood of the oracle, she affirms its strange truth. The "robbers" at the crossroad did indeed act in accordance with the "oracle / rumor." Public "rumor" is simultaneously one with the private "oracle" of Laius's house. Similarly the oracles that appear in the context of public cult (cf. ll. 21, 151ff., 897ff.) show the leader of the *polis* as a lonely bull on the mountain, wandering apart in the "savage woodland" pursued by "every man" of the city (ll. 463–82).

This ode, the first stasimon, focuses a number of the central paradoxes raised by the oracles. We hear it with Teiresias's warning about his "intelligence in the mantic art" ringing in our ears (ll. 461–62). The brilliance of divine speech marked by the opening words of both strophe and antistrophe (l. 463, 473–75) contrasts with the "unspeakable" things committed by the murderer (αρρητ' αρρήτων τελέσαντα, l. 465). The animal imagery and the wild setting contrast both with the human world and with the revered sanctuary: "rock" (ll. 464, 478) refers both to the sacred place and its antithesis, the savage mountain. The loneliness of the bull / murderer is literally "widowhood" (chereuon, l. 479), whereas it is just the opposite, the too close marriage of Oedipus, the gamos agamos, "marriage no-marriage" (l. 1214), which makes the king his bestial opposite, the hunted animal in the savage woodland, wandering with "wretched foot" (l. 479). The metaphor of the ode makes him both the king responsible for the oracles and the guilty criminal exposed by oracles, both a suppliant at Apollo's shrine (through his proxy, Creon) and a wanderer in the wild forest outside that shrine, both inside the city and on the mountain. Parnassus itself faces both ways. It is both a snowy mountain (l. 473), a suggestion of desolation and remoteness, and the "mid-navel of the earth," a center of human concourse and a meeting place between man and God. Hence on the spatial axis of the ploy it occupies the place between Olympus and Cithaeron, the remote mountain of the eternal gods and the mountain which symbolizes the reduction of human life to bestial chaos.

In Oedipus's search Apollo's oracles and the Sphinx's riddles both contrast and converge. The Sphinx exalts, Apollo abases him. The victory over the Sphinx at Thebes is achieved in a lonely encounter analogous to the first visit to Delphi. This victory makes Oedipus king, but also wins him the marriage that puts him outside the human order. In his quarrel with Teiresias Oedipus contrasts his solution to the riddle with the prophetic art (techne: ll. 390–98; cf. l. 380). But these prophecies of Teiresias are "riddling," ainikta (l. 439; cf. ainigma, l. 393), just as the Sphinx is oracular (ll. 1200). The Sphinx propounded a riddle which required "prophecy" (manteia, l. 394; cf. l. 462). Both need "loosing" (cf. l. 392; also ll. 306, 407). According to a tradition preserved in a scholion to Euripides' Phoenissae (l. 1760), "the Sphinx was not a beast (therion), but a propounder of oracles (*chresmologos*) who told the Thebans prophecies that were hard to understand, and she destroyed many of them who misinterpreted the oracles." Riddle and oracle come increasingly to look like mirror-images of one another. Both, when properly "solved" ("loosed"), spell Oedipus's doom.

Oracle and Sphinx stand at the fringes of the human world, the point where divine and human and divine and bestial intersect. Whereas the oracles point upward to a divine, albeit mysterious order, the Sphinx points downward to what is dark, monstrous, subhuman. The oracles mediate between God and man; the Sphinx between man and beast. Half-bestial in form, she is described as "savage" and "raw-eating." She devours her victims and rends her human prey with talons or "savage jaws." She violates the linguistic code in her riddle, biological order in her shape, kin ties in her incestuous parentage (Hesiod, *Theogony*, l. 326ff.), the relation between city and wild in her affliction of the city from her vantage-point on the "Sphinx Mountain" (*Phikeion Oros*) outside or, in other versions, her position on a pillar in the heart of the city. Like Oedipus, her mixed form (lion, bird, woman) involves her in ambiguous locomotion. When the riddle is solved, she plunges from a high place to her death. When Oedipus's riddle is solved, he plunges from the highest to the lowest place in the city (ll. 876–79). In her connections with mountains, she belongs to the savage mountain world of Oedipus's exposure on Cithaeron. Yet her challenge to man is the confusion of human forms with their bestial opposites. This half-beast is a singer of oracles (l. 1200), while the Olympian Apollo leaps like a beast. Her riddle turns man's intelligence against himself, and the solver of her riddle is the example par excellence of profound human ignorance.

As the Sphinx's riddle rests on the equation of two, three, and four, so the killing of Laius involves the coincidence of one and three at the "triple roads," a "double goad" (*dipla kentra*, l. 809), and a mysterious "equality" of "one and many" (l. 845). This evocation of the Sphinx's riddle, however, marks not the victory of human intelligence, but the bestiality released at the no-man's land of the crossroads (ll. 798–813). Oedipus now faces a numerical problem which his intelligence can solve only to his cost.

Like Heracles in the *Trachiniae*, Oedipus protects civilized order by defeating a bestial monster without overcoming the inward dimensions of that monstrosity. Heracles' victory over Nessus to protect marriage ultimately reflects a defeat by his own bestial lust; Oedipus's victory of intelligence over the Sphinx plays into his defeat by his ignorance. As Heracles is vanquished by that aspect of his victory which is still incomplete, so Oedipus is undone by that aspect of the riddle which he has failed to answer. Confrontation with that personal riddle calls forth the "savagery" of his anger (ll. 344, 364) and throws him back into that confusion of god and beast, mind and physical violence which the Sphinx herself embodies.

The Sphinx inverts the mediation between god and man effected by oracles, especially in the realm of language. To the chorus, as we have seen, she is a *chresmodos,* singer of oracles (l. 1200); for presumably her utterances, like the oracle's, are in dactylic hexameter. But she is a "singer" who is "harsh" (l. 36), "of tricky song" (l. 130), a "rhapsode-dog" (l. 391), "hook-taloned maiden singer of riddling oracles" (ll. 1199–1200). Euripides calls her songs "most unmusic" (*Phoen.* 807) and elsewhere dwells on her "musical" aspect. In a fragment of a lost play he describes the riddle as a horrible shrieking whistle. Her song is just the reverse of a civilized art: it enables her to prey upon and destroy a human community. And yet this perverse combination of savagery and civilization parallels that in Oedipus himself. He is the man of intelligence and authority governed by a "savage" temper (l. 344) and "savage" infatuation. The "harmony" he finds in the age of the Shepherd and his own past (*xynaidei,* l. 1113, literally, "sings harmoniously with") leads to the dissonances of his bestial "roar" (l. 1265) and fulfils Teiresias's prophecy that Cithaeron will echo in "harmony" with (*symphonos,* l. 421) those shouts which mark his forfeiture of his place in the city, his loss of the right to the forms of address from its citizens.

Choral lyric could celebrate the "concordant peace," *symphonos hesychia,* of a coherent universe, as Pindar does in the first *Pythian* (ll. 1–40; 71). But the tragic universe has no place for those harmonies. Tragedy, unlike Pindar's "lordly lyre," does not celebrate the unity of city and gods in a secure communal space. Choral song moves from the divine and unknown to the shelter of the familiar rites at the center of the community; tragedy moves from the ritual at the city's center outward to the dangerous unknown of mountain and wild. The very juxtaposition of choral song and the iambics of the suffering protagonist in tragedy sets that communal order over against something else. In like manner the myths of tragedy, unlike the myths of choral lyric, are not exemplary of the city's safe relation to its heroes and gods. The chaos or disorder viewed by Pindar of Bacchylides is itself neutralized by the implicit security of the choral setting. But the tragic performance, like the tragic hero, confronts its own negation: "Why should I dance?" this chorus asks (1. 896). The music of this chorus too has its "bestial double," as it were, in the "harmonies" of Oedipus (ll. 421, 1113) and the choral celebration of the city's opposite, Cithaeron (l. 1093).

Acclaimed for his victory over the "winged maiden" (l. 508), the birdlike Sphinx, Oedipus is defeated by her Olympian opposite and analogue, the oracles which "hover" about the outcast (ll. 481–82) and their interpreter, a reader of bird signs (l. 484, cf. ll. 310, 395, 398). The "bird of good omen," *ornis aisios* (l. 52), which Oedipus brought with him when he defeated the Sphinx, is actually a "bird of ill-omen" (the Greek term has both meanings). Earlier in the prologue, the Theban children are like weak fledglings (ll. 16–17); and in the parode the Thebans themselves appear as birds fleeing a vast fire (ll. 175–78).

These bird images, all underlining the helplessness of men before the supernatural, counterbalance Oedipus's victory over the bird-maiden, the Sphinx. Jubilant at the apparent failure of the oracles, he dismisses "the birds above" (ll. 963–66); but he is mistaken about the father whom he believes "below" the earth (ll. 968). His own ambiguous position between high and low, already underlined by the second stasimon, is made even more dangerous by his being "lifted too high" (l. 914). The chorus, in the first stasimon, "flits about with uncertain hope" (ll. 486–88); but that spatial disorientation becomes more than just foreboding when Oedipus, after the peripety, does not know where he is and wonders at his voice, "flitting about" as if disembodied (ll. 1308–10).

All linked with the oracles, Teiresias, the birds, and the Sphinx locate the ambiguous plane of human truth between animality (the Sphinx) and divine prophecy (Apollo and his "flitting" oracles and birds of omen). The Sphinx is a "singer of oracles" (l. 1200), who yet points down to the beasts. Teiresias is a servant of Apollo, but, like Oedipus, is caught up in an all-too-human anger. He comes in obedience to Oedipus's summons, but will not tell. He conceals as much as he reveals. He is both willing and reluctant, both majestic and irritable; both clear and mysterious; both distant and petty. The manner of his revelation cancels out its credibility. He speaks the truth, but in just such a way that it cannot be received. The context

and the verbal and emotional textures which clothe his message can-
cel the objective truth which it contains. In him language is not
simply the vehicle of truth; it contains truth in its complex, imperfect, riddling human form (cf. l. 439). In him, as in all human truth
in this play, reality is veiled in illusion. To tear off the veil is to bring
destruction as well as "salvation"; but it is the task of the tragic hero
to do exactly this, to stand at the point of "fearful hearing" and press
on (l. 1169; cf. l. 1312).

The two men, Oedipus and Teiresias, reinforce one another in
their blindness-in-vision. They unwillingly collaborate with the god
in demonstrating the imperfection and ambiguity of human truth
and human speech. The shifting status of the birds between Sphinx
and prophet, beastworld and Delphi, is then a function of the play's
larger ambiguities of knowledge and ignorance, the intelligibility or
chaos of the universe. Some of these relationships can be expressed in
the following diagram:

Lower (Beast)	Oedipus	Upper (God)
pharmakos, pollution	defeated by riddles	solver of riddles "godlike man"
Winged maiden = Sphinx		Birds of oracles
Sphinx (beast)	riddles / oracles	Apollo (god)
anger, illusion	Oedipus and Teiresias language as vehicle of confusion / language as instrument of truth	clarity, truth
unintelligibility, chaos	Oedipus proven / Teiresias proven *sophos* in *sophos* in matter of birds interpreting (l. 507ff.) bird-signs	intelligible discourse; orderly universe

Convergence of oracle and Sphinx goes further still. Finding his
identity as both son and husband, brother and father, Oedipus finds
his childhood and his maturity collapsed together—just as they are in
the riddle which he solved in the past and will solve again, with a
profounder and more personal answer, in the action of the play.

"Human life," to quote Geoffrey Hartman, "like a poetic figure,
is an indeterminate middle between overspecified poles always
threatening to collapse it." Oedipus's life parallels the struggle of
language in the play. He attempts to draw forth differentiating order
from his world of fused polarities, to create the space or distance

necessary for significance in a world where that space threatens to disappear under the threat of total nothingness, the zero of meaninglessness or the ungraspable plenum of gods who seem to direct and control everything. "The space Sophocles wrested from the gods," Hartman goes on, "was the very space of human life. That space is illusory, or doomed to collapse as the play focuses on the moment of truth which proves the oracle."

Language, therefore, becomes the microcosm for all of man's means of understanding reality. It reflects the failure of the tools of his intelligence to grasp and order world and self both, to create and maintain "difference" in the face of chaotic sameness and to assert warm familiarity in the face of coldly alien otherness. Oedipus, solver of verbal riddles, is led to defeat by the multiple riddles of his own being until he can find with his own life a deeper answer to the Sphinx's riddle, and that not with words alone.

Until that point is reached, words spoken with deliberate truth say "too much" to be understood (cf. ll. 768–69, 841). Language is "in vain," *maten,* as characters evade or deny plain words (cf. ll. 365 and 1057); but the dismissed *logos* returns with killing force. "Word" and "deed," *logos* and *ergon,* form paradoxical relationships (cf. ll. 219–20, 452, 517). The confused terminology of kinship carries its grim irony throughout the play (ll. 264–65, 928, 1214, 1249ff., 1256, 1403ff.). It becomes a matter of the first importance whether something is "speakable" or "unspeakable" (ll. 301, 465, 993, 1289). Oedipus himself, the authoritative speaker of a public proclamation (cf. ll. 93, 236), comes to utter things unspeakable (ll. 1289, 1313–16) and falls under a ban of speaking or being spoken to (cf. ll. 1437, 239). His first utterances after the peripety are the inarticulate cries *aiai aiai, pheu pheu* (ll. 1307–8). His own voice seems disembodied (l. 1310). Speech is now his only means of recognizing friends or loved ones (cf. ll. 1326, 1472ff.), so that his speech too, like his relation to the rituals and the oracles, moves from the public to the personal sphere.

The basic categories of speech become confused. The riddling Sphinx is a "prophet" (l. 1200), and the oracles are "riddles" (l. 439; cf. ll. 390ff.). The decree of the king (*kerygma,* l. 350, 450) becomes the curse on the one who has spoken it (cf. ll. 744–45). The Corinthian's speech of congratulation (*euepeia,* l. 932) reveals the "reproach" of Oedipus's name and leads to Jocasta's last word of address, the "only word" of her final address, fixing Oedipus forever in his new condition, "unfortunate" (ll. 1071–72).

Logos is here not the glorious achievement celebrated in the *Antigone*'s Ode on Man (l. 353), but something "terrible," *deinon*, in an even darker sense than in the *Antigone*. At the point where "speaking" and "hearing" stand at their peak of "terror" (*deinon*, ll. 1169–70), the *logos* seems to take over almost independently of Oedipus. Sophocles uses a dramatic device analogous to the questioning of Lichas by the Messenger in the *Trachiniae* (ll. 402–33). The chief actor stands on the sidelines, a momentarily silent witness, for the most crucial *logos* of his life; and the solving of his riddle goes on, momentarily, without the direct participation of the great riddle-solver himself.

The deepest irony of Oedipus's relation to language lies, of course, in his name. That primary and fundamental act of communication, the naming of a child in the House, is not a name, a *logos*, but the scars left by his "yoking" on the mountain. His name is a reproach (*oneidos*, ll. 1035–36). Oedipus "called the glorious" will give his name to Cithaeron (ll. 1451–52), henceforth linked with him. Nothing could be less justified than this nameless ruler's pride in what he is "called" (l. 8). To learn the truth of his name is, as he says at the end, to pronounce "the names of all the evils that there are" (ll. 1284–85).

By learning and accepting the truth of his name, Oedipus, like the hero of the *Odyssey*, reestablishes the structures of differentiation over the randomness of the animal world. But the recreation of civilization in tragedy is far more precarious than it is in epic. The end of Oedipus's quest is to fracture the "seeming" unity of his life and his language into its bipolar reality. He is not just "king," but also scapegoat; not just husband, but also son; not just *tyrannos*, but also *basileus;* and so on. It is his tragic destiny to replace apparent oneness with binary and ternary terms. He is the quintessentially Sophoclean tragic hero in his extreme division between appearance and reality, outward and inward truth. The riddle as the cancellation or confusion of verbal differentiation parallels the other cancellations of differences which make up the moral and intellectual clarity of our world. It is the problem of the one being equal to many, as Oedipus says (ll. 845–47); and for Sophocles, as for Plato, the relation of the One to the Many is the focal point for man's understanding of himself and the universe.

Violating the limits of speech, Oedipus also violates those of silence. At the crossroads he fails to utter the humanizing word that might have saved Laius and himself. "These things will come even if I conceal them in silence," Teiresias warns. "Then should you speak to me of what will come," is Oedipus's reply (l. 342). There are some things which are "unspeakable," but Oedipus is no respecter of these constraints. Only Creon, the man of good sense, the untragic figure, knows how "to keep knowledge where I have no knowledge" (l. 609). He makes this remark in his futile self-defence, and repeats it, in a very different context, at the end of the play (l. 1519). He would "give an account," *logon didonai,* in the reasonable atmosphere of forensic debate (ll. 583–84); but his attempt, like Teiresias's more spirited attempt, fails before the "savage" wrath of Oedipus.

Confounded or puzzled by silence, Oedipus forcibly elicits speech. He repeats the pattern four times: first with the chorus in his decree about keeping silent (ll. 233–43); next with Teiresias (l. 340ff.), whom he compels to repeat his fearful words not once, but three times (ll. 359–65), "making trial of words" (l. 360); then with Jocasta (l. 1056ff., especially 1074–75); and finally with the old herdsman, where he actually uses physical torture (l. 1153). Yet the mysterious silence of the gods cannot be forced before its time, and it is this which defies all of Oedipus's most strenuous efforts. "How, how could the furrows of your father have borne you in silence (*siga*), miserable man, for so long?" (ll. 1210–12).

II

With the disintegration or confusion of the communicative function of language, the basic relation to physical reality is threatened. Speaking, hearing, and seeing are no longer taken for granted. It is as if the world of Oedipus contracts from his dominion over Thebes to the mountainside where the exposed infant is doomed to cry without being heard, without learning human speech.

Early in the play "speaking" and "hearing" (*kluein, akouein*) belong to the ruler's communication with his subjects: he speaks and they hear or obey (cf. ll. 216, 235; cf. also ll. 84, 91, 294–95). In the encounter with Teiresias the double function of "hearing" and "speaking" as cognition and communication begins to break apart. Accustomed to having others "hear" him, he will not "hear" Teiresias (cf. l. 429). "Blind in ears and mind and eyes," he calls the prophet (l. 371), but Teiresias at once turns the line back upon Oedipus himself (ll. 372–73). The three terms correspond almost exactly to

Oedipus's reply to the first mention of Laius (l. 105): "I *know* by *hearing*, but I never *saw* him." In the first stasimon striking synaesthetic imagery combines sight and sound to describe the words of the Delphic oracle: the oracle (*phama*) appears and "flashes forth" (*elampse*, ll. 473–75). The chorus would "see an upright word" (l. 505; cf. also l. 187). But neither sight nor hearing helps Oedipus. His refusal to "hear" plays an important role in the scene with Creon (cf. ll. 543–44). In the next scene, with Jocasta, it becomes crucial for him to ascertain just what has been heard (ll. 729, 850), until he arrives at the point of "dreadful hearing" from which there is no return (ll. 1169–70).

Having dwelt in a world of illusionary seeing and hearing, of mistaken perception as well as false or incomplete communication, Oedipus now finds that he has no desire for the organs of cognition (l. 1224): "What deeds will you *hear,* what deeds will you *see?"* cries the Messenger at the beginning of his description of Jocasta's death and Oedipus's self-blinding. "Why then," Oedipus asks a little later, "should I want sight since when I saw there was nothing joyful to behold" (ll. 1334–35). If he could, he would have closed up the channels of hearing as well as sight "that I might be blind and hear nothing, for to house one's thought (*phrontida . . . oikein*) outside of evils is sweet" (ll. 1384–90). The man who lost in infancy, and now in adulthood, the house (*oikos*) where the senses are trained to perception and communication, would now "house" (*oikein*) his mind outside of its sufferings by giving up all perception of reality. This act not only fulfils Teiresias's prophecy (cf. ll. 371 and 1389), but also has a more fundamental meaning, referring to man's existential and cognitive reality both: cast out of the house, having no "place" among men, Oedipus does not "know where" (cf. ll. 1309–11). His rhetoric acts out, inwardly and physically, both the parents' rejection of the child and the city's ritual expulsion of the *pharmakos* or pollution. His desire to shut out physical reality recapitulates his original expulsion from the human world and also corresponds to his newly discovered status as the pollution who cannot be shown to earth or sky (ll. 1425–28).

Yet Oedipus does not sever his bond with life. Touch and hearing remain, and are intimately linked with his human feelings of grief, pity, and joy. He can "hear" the chorus's voice in the darkness (ll. 1325–26). When he hears his "dear ones weeping," he realizes that Creon has "pitied" him "knowing," as Creon adds, his "joy" (*terpsin*) in his children (ll. 1471–77). He seems to repeat the gesture of the old servant who "touched the hand" of Jocasta in a suppliant's request to be sent away from the house, "out of sight of the town" (ll. 760–62; cf. ll. 1437ff., 1449ff.) But, a little later in this scene, Oedipus, the polluted outcast, asks to "touch the hands" of his dear ones and to "weep over his woes" with them (l. 1466ff.). Reduced to this groping of hands, he hits the rock bottom of his humanity, still left to him in this relation of touch and hearing. The house is his curse, but it is the only space which can receive him now as seen and heard (ll. 1429–31); and it is still the place where he, the land's pollution, can exchange touch.

Oedipus does not abandon his house as his house abandoned him. Though he is "made equal to his children" by the incest consequent on that earlier expulsion from the house (l. 425), he asks that his children not be "made equal" to his sufferings (l. 1507). Destroyed by the ambiguities of speech, he can now experience another quality of civilized speech in the friendly voice of the chorus who do not forsake him (ll. 1325–26) and the voices of his children whom Creon allows him to "hear" (l. 1472). Time and knowledge, which are destructive while Oedipus was ignorant of his place in the house, can create understanding and compassion when Creon grants him the meeting with his daughters because he "knew of old" Oedipus's delight in them. Darkness and groping touch with hand (l. 1466) or staff replace the apparent sight and "scepter" of the king. But at the same time a tender exchange of speech within a house which is now truly, if grimly, his own partially fills the gap between regal command and cry on the wild mountainside. In the dramatic reversal from strength to weakness, from sceptred king to blind beggar with his staff, Oedipus gives his final answer to the riddle of the Sphinx. Oedipus the King becomes Oedipus the man.

Oedipus becomes a second Teiresias. Yet he has the inner sight of his blindness not as a gift of the gods, but as the hard acquisition of his human experience and suffering. In his seeing blindness he discerns not the future, like the old prophet, but the meaning of his past and the reality of his own condition of strength-in-weakness in the present.

At the end of the play Oedipus's imperfect, proud "knowing" ripens into the "knowledge that he has been set apart for a unique destiny." He discerns and responsibly accepts the fact that his life has a shape, a pattern which it must fulfil, formed by the interlocking of internal and external determinants, character and "chance" both. After crying out that he would dwell on the mountains which his parents chose as his tomb (ll. 1451–53), he pulls back abruptly and makes his deepest statement of "knowing" in the play (ll. 1455–58):

> But yet I know (*oida*) this much, that no disease or anything else can destroy me, for I would not have been saved from death except for some terrible suffering. Wherever my fated portion (*moira*) goes, let it go.

It is at this point, after facing the possibility that his life may be a cruel joke played upon him by malignant gods that Oedipus turns to Creon and asks about his children. In that gesture he finally leaves the bare mountainside which his own parents gave him instead of a house and turns back for the touch and the speech of those remaining to him in his own shattered house.

The pollution is still there. It is not overborne, as it is by the inward innocence of Heracles in Euripides' *Heracles Mad* or by Oedipus's own certainty of his place in the gods' will in the *Coloneus*. Against the enormity of the pollution this last gesture of human contact and human love is, by its very naturalness, momentous.

Only when Oedipus joins the two ends of his life, infancy and adulthood, and becomes the incestuous parricide along with father and king, does his life begin to make sense as part of a tragic, yet intelligible pattern. At that point a design becomes visible which embraces his exposure on the mountain, his victory over the Sphinx, his consequent rule over Thebes, and his desire to be cast out upon the mountain. All the parts taken individually at any point and grasped in the totality of their interconnection exemplify his essential greatness-in-nothingness, strength-in-weakness.

Only man spans such conflicting opposites; and only man, therefore, has a tragic destiny, which includes also the capacity to bring that coexistence of opposites to consciousness. Oedipus answers and lives out, knowingly, in his own life, the riddle of the Sphinx, which is the riddle both of man's being in time and of his paradoxical union of the one and the many simultaneously. The months which Oedipus says defined him great and small are truly proven his "kindred" (ll. 1082–83) because time and the changes which time brings not only mark man's tragic bondage to death, but also the precariousness and the painfulness of self-knowledge.

Moving from king to pollution, from seeing to blind, from rich house to the savage mountain of the monstrous birth and rejected outcast, Oedipus becomes, even more deeply than Teiresias, a constellation of contradictions and opposites. He realizes his identity not as a stable unity, but as a juncture of polarities. Replacing the blind seer as the paradigm of man's tragic knowledge, he joins these oppositions in conscious and agonized union rather than unconscious coincidence. Oedipus seeks the murderer of Laius, whom he fears as his own, and finds himself. His sufferings in the play constitute a far more significant "answer" to the Sphinx's riddle than the one which he so confidently gave outside Thebes in his youth. By living out his answer, he becomes a more authentic civilizing hero, the bearer of the tragic meaning of civilization for men. Prometheus, the archetypal culture-hero, gave men "blind hopes" along with the arts of civilization so that they could not foresee their death. Oedipus tears away the veil and by his self-chosen blindness gives men sight.

"That we are set into a 'blind destiny,' dwell within it," Rilke once wrote, "is, after all in a way the condition of our sight. . . . Only through the 'blindness' of our fate are we really deeply related to the wonderful muffledness of the world, that is, with what is whole, vast, and surpassing us." For Sophocles, however, that "muffledness" is not "wonderful," but terrible-and-wonderful, *deinon.* To exemplify in his own life the mystery of existence is not a blessing, but a misfortune, a curse. Yet only through that blindness can the hero know the vast life of the universe in all its strange, remote workings.

Oedipus's fate in the orchestra mirrors back to the members of the audience their own experience, in the theater, of nothingness before time and change. As they watch the performance, they too pass from blind seeing to seeing blindness, from the comfortable certitudes of daily life to the shaken awareness of how fragile these certitudes are, how thin the film between reality and illusion. They too, in firm control of their lives, are, like Oedipus, "struck" or "shaken," *ekpeplegmenos* (l. 922), a word used by Sophocles' contemporaries to describe both intense aesthetic and emotional reactions. Each member of the audience, joined but also isolated in the silent crowd, celebrating a festival but also involved in the sufferings of the masked actor, temporarily loses his identity, his secure definition by house, position, friends, and becomes, like Oedipus, nameless and placeless, weighing the light accidents of birth, fortune, status above the void of nonbeing. Like all tragic art this play above all reveals the fragility of those structures—ritual, social, moral—which enclose it and are the sources of its life. In every sense, as Knox observes, personal, historical, communal, "the audience which watched Oedipus in the theater of Dionysus was watching itself."

Yet what ultimately emerges from the *Oedipus Rex* is not a sense of total chaos and despair, but a quality of heroism in the power of self-knowledge. "No other mortal except myself can bear my sufferings," Oedipus says near the end. The verb *pherein*, "bear," "endure," is a leitmotif of the play. Like everything which touches Oedipus intimately it spans the two poles of weakness and strength. Both Teiresias and Jocasta, in different ways, urge him to "bear life easily" (cf. ll. 320–21 and 982–83). But by destiny and by temperament Oedipus does not exist in the middle ground where such "bearing" is possible. He has, as Creon tells him, a "nature most painful to bear" (ll. 675–76) and "bears ill" the half-knowledge of his encounter with Laius (cf. l. 770).

In a life where so much seems to have been "chance" or randomness (cf. Jocasta's *eikei* in l. 979), Oedipus not only discerns pattern, but creates pattern. His capacity to "bear," *pherein,* is connected with his determination to discover the shape which his life has within the mysterious order, or disorder, of the gods, to discern the coherence between the inner nature and the outward event, between the beginning and the end, the suffered and the inflicted injury. Whereas earlier Oedipus angrily rejected the "pains" (*pemonai,* l. 363) which Teiresias had foretold for him, at the end he "chooses" them as his own (*authairetoi pemonai,* l. 1230ff.) and strikes with his own hand (l. 1331ff.). These "self-chosen pains" answer the "savage pain" of Jocasta (l. 1073ff.), who cannot face the suffering contained in her destiny and also the disordered pains of Oedipus's violent emotional oscillations when he "lifts up his spirit too much with pains of all sorts" (*lypai pantoiai,* ll. 914–15).

For Oedipus, more than for any Greek hero, ontogeny recapitulates phylogeny; the hero is both individual and mythic paradigm. Oedipus does not solve the ultimate riddle, the meaning of the gods who remain as remote as the stars with which Oedipus, in the first step of the exile which will henceforth be his life's pattern, measures his distance from Corinth (l. 779). But he follows this pattern to the end, and completes it, as symbol and paradigm, by a self-inflicted suffering. To search for and accept his hidden origins and his darker self is to essay anew the riddle of the Sphinx, that is, enter the tragic path of self-knowledge and force language too to the same tragic search and self-questioning.

The Language of Oedipus

John Gould

> *World, world, O world!*
> *But that thy strange mutations make us hate thee,*
> *Life would not yield to age.*
> King Lear 4.1.10–12

Colin Macleod, in a footnote to "Politics and the Oresteia," speaks of Sophoclean drama being concerned not just with the lonely individual but "by the same token . . . [with] his estrangement from his fellow-men or his precarious place among them." It is with an aspect of that "estrangement" and "precariousness" that I shall be concerned in this essay.

About Sophocles' *King Oedipus,* apart from a general acknowledgment that it is one of the masterworks of Greek tragedy, we are a long way from any sort of critical agreement. Some of the reasons at least for this state of affairs are not hard to find. Ever since Aristotle, the play has suffered from being treated as the paradigm case of a Greek tragedy, so that whatever qualities it was thought necessary that a Greek tragedy should have, all were of necessity found here. If tragedies were about tragic flaws, then Oedipus must have his flaw. It is as if sometimes the criticism of Sophocles' play gets caught up in tramlines of argument from which it is astonishingly difficult to extricate the discussion. But of these temptations to misread the play, I mean to say little or nothing, since they have been lucidly (and, one might have hoped, finally) dealt with by E. R. Dodds in his classic essay "On Misunderstanding the *Oedipus Rex*." A different sort of difficulty for the critic and one more intrinsic to the play's meaning arises from the fact that it is a play of which the theatergoer's experience is very different from that of the reader of the play-text. For the latter, it seems all too easy to restructure the play in the memory according to a logical or a chronological sequence which is quite different from the one Sophocles has given it, and then to draw inferences from the remembered structure that are quite alien to the play as Sophocles wrote it for performance.

These are certainly things we have to be careful about, but further and more importantly still (since here we move close to the heart of the problems Sophocles' play sets us), *King Oedipus* is a play whose qualities of inscrutability and of pervasive irony quickly come to complicate any critical discussion. It is a play of transformations in which things turn into other things as we watch, where meanings and implications seem to be half-glimpsed beneath the surface of the text only to vanish as we try to take them in, and where ironical resemblances and reflections abound to confuse our response. Richmond Lattimore pointed out some years since that the basic structure of the action is that of the foundling discovered, an action more familiar to us as it is normally realised in the comic mode, as for instance in the happy-ever-after world of Menander or of Roman comedy, or in *The Importance of Being Earnest*. We do not respond to King Oedipus as if it were a comedy only because of our familiarity with genre, because, as Northrop Frye puts it, "comedy prevents heroes from marrying their sisters or their mothers"; nonetheless, the effect of such ironical associations of genre is to render the play vulnerable to multiple possibilities of misunderstanding. The most evident, perhaps, are those which stem from the resemblance of *King Oedipus* to a detective story. Some misreadings of the play provoked by *that* resemblance, notably Philip Vellacott's, remind one irresistibly of Thurber's story "The Macbeth Murder Mystery."

Sophoclean irony is central to his meaning and it is disturbing, but it is not the irony of a morally uncommitted observer; still less is it a kind of superior mockery of the moral weakness or rashness of the agents in the story. It is, to quote Lionel Trilling writing of irony in Jane Austen, "primarily . . . a method of comprehension. It perceives the world through an awareness of its contradictions, paradoxes and anomalies." Of course, to summon up Jane Austen when one speaks of irony in Sophocles is to risk confusion. There is a world of difference between Jane Austen's ironic reinforcement of social values and Sophocles' cosmic and subversive tragic irony, with its terrifying power of coincidence, its capacity for mutation and reversal, of every kind, of sense, of value, of identity. But there is also an important point of sameness in that, as with Jane Austen's irony, it is practised upon ourselves as audience as much as upon the characters of the play. For the play encourages us constantly to make connections and to draw out implications that in the end we are forced to reassess, to question and perhaps abandon.

Let me take an example: the moment, almost central in the play, in which Iokasta emerges from the palace to offer garlands and incense to Apollo and to pray for resolution of anxiety and for the removal of *agos* (ll. 911–23). Her action is followed, without pause for taking of breath, by the entry of a shepherd with news of the death of Oedipus's adoptive father, Polybus, the king of Corinth, news which Oedipus takes to be lifting of the cloud of fear which has haunted him, and confirmation of the supposition, put to him moments before by Iokasta, that the purported truths of oracles are worthless and not to be regarded. But the immediate conjunction of prayer and arrival has suggested to many readers, and one might guess to many in audiences of the play, that the second is consequent upon the first, that Apollo *answers* Iokasta's prayers with the news from Corinth, an answer that presents itself as doubly ironical in view both of Iokasta's earlier disbelief in the professions of seers, and of the discovery now almost instantly to be made that Polybus was not, after all, Oedipus's natural father. Iokasta, with Oedipus's almost whole-minded agreement, concludes that chance is in control of human experience.

We seem led to infer that she is wrong, that Apollo is at work and that Sophocles structures his play so as to make us see this. And yet there is nothing that happens either now or later in the play to confirm that inference, or to make it certain that, mistaken though Iokasta and Oedipus clearly are in their perceptions of things, they may not be right in this at least, in their belief that Apollo is not steering the course of things to an end which men can foresee, by bird-skill or by the utterance of oracles; perhaps that he is not steering them at all.

For this incident should bring home to us a crucial and central truth about *King Oedipus:* the divine powers, their acts and motives, are hidden, both from us and from the characters in this play. We do not see them, as we do so often in the world of Euripidean tragedy, in Aeschylus's *Eumenides* or in Sophocles' own *Ajax;* we sense them present and we sense them act, but we must infer their presence and their activity from such indications as ordinary men may have of the involvement of superhuman powers in their experience. That is, from the occurrence of uncanny and significant events, from oracular utterances and from the riddling words of seers.

We make our inferences as we watch the characters make theirs. Some of theirs, we know, are wrong, but we are not quite ever in a position to be certain that we always know which or that our own are well-founded. And in judging their inferences and making ours, we have to remember all along that oracles (like dreams) most often turn out to mean something other than what they seem to say; that riddles challenge and tantalize half-mockingly; that, though they are not nonsense, they seem purposefully and systematically to defy sense and do not yield their sense without a struggle; and that occurrences may have no further meaning beyond that they occur. Not every man has the skill to steer a true course between assuming a meaning grasped that events will prove mistaken, and dismissing events and words prematurely as without significance. The characters, we see, do not have this skill (save only Teiresias), but Sophocles' play challenges not only them but also us, the audience, to make the right connections; it chafes and teases and tantalizes from the start. And we have to be ready for that.

In this essay, I want to approach the play's meaning through two oppositions defined by its stage action and its language: the first between the language of Oedipus (and in counterpoint with it that of Kreon) on the one hand and the language of Teiresias on the other; the second an opposition of place, in the categorization of space, between the *poleis* of Thebes and Corinth, and the space "outside," the mountainsides and tracks and crossroads of Oedipus's other world. I shall argue that these two oppositions are parallel and complementary to each other and that together they structure that sense of the "otherness" of divinity which controls our deeper responses to the play and causes us to see the action of *King Oedipus* as an action of man and god, however indecipherable we feel its motivations or its moral tendency to be.

A play is, in a way that determines our response to its meaning, a sequential experience; our response is shaped through the duration of its performance. So I will begin at the beginning and try to elucidate our response *seriatim* to what we watch.

The opening of the play presents us with a gathering of suppli-

ants (the old and the young, no women, no fully adult males, so that
Oedipus is, at once, magnified and isolated), seated at the altars of
the gods before Oedipus's palace. Offstage, we learn, other suppliants sit at other altars throughout the city. The people of Thebes
have judged that the gods are angry, since their city is caught in a
"bloody swell" of sickness, stillbirths among humans and animals,
blight on the crops and plague deaths spreading throughout the population. The scene, as we see it, is focused upon Oedipus, who,
significantly, speaks before he is addressed. His opening words, the
first of the play, form a question as to the meaning of the ritual he
sees before him. They are followed by a statement of other ritual
sounds and smells which fill the *polis* that he cannot see, and of his
concern to learn their sense. His calm authority is overwhelming and
majestic (the people of Thebes are his "children"), his sense of obligation to the *polis* is marked in every word of his speech, which
culminates in the expression of human pity as its keynote (l. 13). But
on what does Oedipus's authority rest? There is a crucial uncertainty
here. Is it that he is king of Thebes, the holder of the community's
secular power and the representative of its norms and laws, or that he
has particular and special affinity with the divine powers that now
seem to control events at Thebes? The priest of Zeus, who is spokes-
man for the suppliants, is explicit in specifying Oedipus's authority,
but his words are not unambiguous. The suppliants, he asserts, are
seated at the hearth not because they judge Oedipus "ranked equal
with the gods, / but as the first of men both in the ordinary chances
of life / and in encounters with divinity" (ll. 31–34). The priest cites
Oedipus's rescue of Thebes from the "tribute of the hard singer," the
Sphinx. That was judged to be done "with the aid of god." Is Oedipus then bound in some way to divinity? Perhaps. But Oedipus
himself answers with words of human distress and shared anxiety, as
the father of a troubled people; he asks questions as to the meaning
of religious acts, as if they are outside his knowledge. His response,
significantly, is the response of a secular authority in realms beyond
its competence, conscious of not knowing what the gods intend; it is
to send (indeed to have sent) a trusted envoy to Apollo's oracle at
Delphi and to await word of the god, ready to act on whatever the
god reveals. At the end of this scene we are left still uncertain as to
the nature of Oedipus's relationship with divinity.

Kreon, the envoy, enters but before he speaks the god's words
there is a political issue to be determined: whether to speak publicly,

in earshot of the gathered Thebans, or in private council inside the palace. Kreon implies a preference for privacy; Oedipus decides, unhesitatingly, for public disclosure. The god plainly commands the removal, by death or banishment, of one who is polluting the land of Thebes, the killer of its former king, Laios, and Oedipus reacts by calling an assembly of the people of Kadmos, to hear his proclamation and to witness the beginning of his investigation into this old crime. Before the proclamation comes the entry-song of the chorus, an extended prayer to the gods of Thebes. It is full of religious fears and hopes, horror at the terrifying and uncanny speed, like that of a fire borne before the wind or like the sudden flight of a flock of migrating birds, with which the sickness spreads and the deaths become too numerous to count, and of appeals to all the gods of Thebes to "appear," to bring their aid, the "bright face of their protection." The hope is of light from the divine powers, imagined as coming with gold and torches in the dark.

The prayer ends and it is Oedipus who answers, directly and with some effect of strangeness, as if it were he who was addressed, with a proclamation excommunicating the killer from all communion in the sacred rituals of Thebes, and from all public or private forms of association with the citizens of Thebes, "whose throne and power I wield." The language of the proclamation must be understood by the Athenian audience on the analogy of that of the quasi-ritual procedures of Athenian homicide law, the law of Drakon, which involved a twofold declaration, by the kinsmen of the dead man and by the King archon, requiring the killer to "be excluded from the recognised things," which embraced the rituals of sprinkling with holy water and of libation, prayer and sacrifice that make up the terms of Oedipus's proclamation here. Oedipus, of course, speaks as king of Thebes, as his words underline, not as kinsman of the dead Laios; he speaks as citizen (astos) to citizens, as possessing the power that Laios once possessed and as inheritor of his social role as husband and as father. Even the curse he utters against those who refuse to carry out the terms of his proclamation is uttered, it seems, as having the approval of the people of Kadmos. There is no suggestion that the imprecation is of one whose power to curse comes directly from personal affinity with the gods. This scene, then, reinforces our sense of Oedipus as the representative of a secular power and the upholder of a secular community and its laws; so, even more strikingly, does the scene that follows.

For Teiresias, who enters now, does have such a personal affinity with the divine powers, seemingly in pointed contrast with Oedipus; his blindness is the mark of it, he is given the title "lord" (*anax*) in explicit and symmetrical association with Apollo. He is known by the chorus to share Apollo's vision, and Oedipus speaks to him in a heightened version of the language of supplication and ritual self-abasement (l. 326f.) that the priest of Zeus had used in addressing him. Oedipus's appeal to Teiresias is framed in the language of obligation to the *polis* (he uses the word five times in forty lines) whose "protector and rescuer" he is asked to be. Teiresias's reply, implying refusal to speak, is received by Oedipus with astonishment and incomprehension, as outright disloyalty to the *polis* which has brought him up and to its norms and rules (ll. 322–23), even as insult (l. 340), treason and deliberate destruction of the community (l. 331). Oedipus is alienated from Teiresias precisely in the measure that Teiresias totally fails to acknowledge his membership of and debt to the political community: their words and visions do not meet.

The opening scenes of *King Oedipus,* I am suggesting, present us with an image of Oedipus as a political figure, a human king whose power derives from the community he rules, whose perceptions and whose feelings are indissolubly bound up with the experience of the men of Thebes, whose language he speaks and where though a latecomer, he belongs. He is, it seems, of his city, a citizen among citizens, as Teiresias, who denies himself even the status of *metoikos* and claims instead to be Apollo's slave (ll. 410–11), is not. The opposition in language between Oedipus and Teiresias (human / divine; secular / sacred; political / apolitical) could not be more sharply drawn. The only counterindication lies in the words ambiguously used of Oedipus and to him by the priest of Zeus ("not as ranked equal with the gods, but as the first of men . . . in encounters with divinity"), and perhaps in the ritual act of supplication itself. But neither is more than a hint, a tantalising suggestion of something that does not quite fit the rest of what we are given on which to build our image of the king—and neither is unambiguous. Morever, we are reinforced in our hypothetical construction of the dramatic personality of Oedipus along the lines I am suggesting because only such a reading of his mind and language enables us to respond straightforwardly to his reactions to Teiresias, and later to Kreon, in the scenes that follow. For Oedipus's response to Teiresias's accusation that it is *he* who is polluting Thebes and who stands excommunicated by his own proclamation, he who is the killer of Laios, is to infer at once a political conspiracy to displace him from power, and to fix on Kreon as the beneficiary and hence the author of the plot. The best commentary on Oedipus's reaction is Otanes' characterisation of the *tyrannos* (Herodotus 3.80), and the countercharge makes political sense. Teiresias, evidently, is lying, for no motive of his own that could explain his acts, and must have been put up to it; Kreon is the likeliest to gain if Oedipus can be hounded out of Thebes through the weight of Teiresias's accusation and his status as seer. Nor indeed, when Kreon enters, does he dispute the inference that Teiresias is lying nor that he has been suborned; he merely offers reasons why the suborning cannot be *his* work. And they are good, sound reasons; they too make political sense, since Kreon, like Oedipus, possesses a political mind, and speaks the language of politics. His thoughts and reactions are those of a political animal, who calculates his own good in relation to the community, and to his standing and authority within it, and expects others to do the same. He is appalled at Oedipus's accusation precisely because it threatens that standing, and in rebutting it he addresses himself to the chorus (characteristically) as "fellow citizens" (l. 512). When he retorts, in answer to Oedipus's appeal to "the *polis*," for witness and support that "I too have my place in the *polis*" (l. 630), we believe him. He and Oedipus speak the same language, a language which puts both beyond the range of understanding such as Teiresias's whose world is alien.

If we approach the opening scenes of the play in this way, as the whole tenor of the words of Oedipus seems to suggest we should, then there will be nothing puzzling (and in performance, I suggest, there *is* nothing puzzling) in Oedipus's response to the remainder of the taunts that Teiresias directs at him. The accusation that he killed Laios he understands and responds to; it makes sense, and it could have a meaning and a motivation that Oedipus can grasp without surrendering his sense of himself. But thereafter Teiresias's words take on the opacity of riddle; they have a compassion of syntax and an echoing resonance that seem to baffle sense, to hint at meanings which, if they exist, must lie somewhere in another realm of discourse, a world behind or beyond the apparent reference of the words themselves. For they mean either nothing or too much; to understand them Oedipus would indeed have to surrender his sense of himself—and of Teiresias. For Teiresias's words speak the double-

meaning language of oracles and seers, but Oedipus has already inferred, on the best of evidence, that Teiresias does not possess the
skill and mind of the seer; his pretensions are false, rooted, it now
appears, in no special affinity with the gods, as the experience of the
Sphinx should have revealed to all long since. And Oedipus sees
himself as having solved the Sphinx's riddle by "mind" (l. 398) as
Themistocles read the language of Apollo (Herodotus 7.141–44), and
not by any seer's skill. So there is no way that Oedipus could read
these riddles while he holds to his knowledge of what he and Teiresias
are; without, that is, in some sense abandoning his mind and speaking another language. Without, one might almost say, going out of
his mind—as in a moment he is going to do.

In reading the Teiresias scene in this way I am following the lead
of Oliver Taplin. We are the more prepared to read it in this light by
Oedipus's own words a few lines earlier (ll. 437–39): in reply to
Oedipus's unambiguous question, "What human gave me birth?,"
Teiresias had replied, "This day will give you birth and will destroy
you," to which Oedipus in despair had cried in reply: "How everything you say is riddles and unclear!" But I am well aware that not
all critics of the play read the scene as I have just done. Indeed, for the
most recent editor of the play, R. D. Dawe, the scene stands out as
the most conspicuous of the "sequence of improbabilities" that cause
him (and, he suggests, other among "the more conscientious students of Sophocles") "misgivings" and "much worry." Dawe's
reading of the scene is instructive because it is an exemplary instance
of how an approach to the language of a dramatic text based on false
premises leads inevitably to distortion, even to radical distortion, of
the text's meaning. Here is Dawe's translation of Teiresias's speech at
lines 447–62:

> I have said what I came to say, and now I am going home
> unmoved by fear in your presence. You cannot hurt me,
> and I will tell you why. The man that you have been
> looking for all this time, with all your threats and procla-
> mations about the murder of Laios, that man is here. He is
> supposed to be a stranger living in our midst, but in time
> he will be found to be a native Theban, a turn of events
> that will give him no pleasure. He *who once had* vision *will
> be* blind; *no longer* wealthy, he *will be* a mendicant feeling
> the ground before him with his staff as he traverses a for-

eign land. And everyone will know that he is both *the* brother and *the* father of his own children, *the* son and husband of the woman that gave him birth, *the man* who killed his father and *climbed into an empty bed*. Now go and think about that for a while, and if you find that I have spoken false, let all men hereafter say that I know nothing of prophecy.

The words and phrases I have italicised represent more or less serious distortions of the meaning of Sophocles' Greek, all of them tending in the same direction, that is, towards draining Teiresias's words of their uncanny resonance and eery, tantalising impenetrability and rendering them flat, unchallenging and unequivocal. For instance, where Dawe writes "he who once had vision will be blind; no longer wealthy, he will be a mendicant," Sophocles' Greek has (literally) "out of sighted, blind and a beggar in place of (or "in return for") wealthy." The explicit reference to temporal sequence is simply not there in the Greek, and other more teasing overtones, of mutation, reciprocity and exchange, are. So too with the inserted articles in Dawe's version, where the Greek (once more literally) says: "he will be displayed associating with his own children, the same man, brother and father, to her from whom he took his birth (or "nature") son and husband and of his father seed-sharer and killer"—nothing at all to warrant "climbed into the empty bed." And Teiresias's challenge to Oedipus to "go inside and reckon these things up," a provocative challenge to Oedipus's pretensions as calculator and reasoner (as Bernard Knox pointed out long since), is wholly lost in "thinking about that for a while."

Now I do not want to suggest for a moment that Dawe's distortions of Teiresias's words are deliberate or even conscious manipulation of the test; I am sure they are not. They are the more instructive, I suspect, for not being. They stem from Dawe's certainty that he knows what Teiresias's meaning is in what he says to Oedipus and from his desire to help him realise it, and of course in one sense he does. What is *signified* by Teiresias's words is indeed conveyed to us in Dawe's translation, but his words and their effect are not, and it is of absolutely overriding critical importance that in responding to this scene it is to Teiresias's *words* and their resonance that we respond. We shall simply fail to understand the scene, as we shall fail to understand Oedipus and the whole meaning of Sophocles' play, if we allow *our* knowledge of Oedipus's circumstances and origin to come between us and Teiresias's words. We have to read the scene with Oedipus's mind, the mind that Sophocles has given him, and not with some attributed awareness.

If we respond as we should (and must), then we shall see, of course, that there is a coherence to the political world of the opening scenes of *King Oedipus* and to the way that human behavior is perceived in it that is threatened but not exposed by the language of Teiresias. It all makes sense, the world of the play as it appears through the eyes and in the language of Oedipus. And yet it is wrong; we *know* it is wrong. Oedipus did not solve the riddle of the Sphinx by "mind," by getting it right, by luck or by precision of aim (*kuresas*); like the priest of Zeus, we know (we *think* we know) that it was by the presence and aid of a god, some god. I have said that the play teases us, and of course it does so because we bring to it, inevitably, some knowledge of Oedipus that Sophocles, seemingly, had denied to Oedipus himself, some sense of the uncanny, awesome strangeness that surrounds him and of which he seems wholly unaware: that, precisely, is Sophocles' "irony." So far in the play only a scattering of uncertain hints have disturbed the coherence of Oedipus's world and the cool rationality of his language. But now we are at the hinging point of the play.

Sophocles has made this moment (ll. 631–96), about which the play turns, a little before halfway through its course, elaborately formal, even operatic. Its formal structure marks a separation from everything that has gone before, and from most that is to come; only the entry of Oedipus after his self-blinding offers something of the same richness of texture. And the effect is not only to give this scene a peculiar sharpness of dramatic focus but also to cause it to act as bridge between two worlds, the secular, political world of the play's opening scenes and the increasingly demonic, steadily more terrifying world into which Oedipus now moves—or to which he now finds himself returning. Iokasta enters upon the quarrel of Oedipus and Kreon; for the first time in the play, three actors are present, as well as the chorus. Almost at once, speech and song are used to interweave all of them in exchanges of a complex and unusual symmetry. Oedipus is forced to give way, to make a political decision he believes absolutely wrong, under the pressure of urgent, political appeals to put first the needs of the *polis,* to accept the sanctity of an oath and to revoke the sentence of exile or death uttered against

Kreon. The chorus, leading citizens of Thebes (and not, we should note, Iokasta) press the case upon him and Oedipus yields. Kreon goes. At once the formal tightness of the scene relaxes into spoken dialogue. Iokasta turns to Oedipus, to ask him to explain the origin of his bitter quarrel with her brother. And immediately the ground of Oedipus, on which he stands, begins to slip beneath his feet.

Significantly, the words that cause the first giddying panic in Oedipus's mind are prosaic, ordinary words of place, of a "place where three carriage-roads meet (l. 716)," the "division in the road (l. 733)," as Iokasta expands upon her first passing allusion, where tracks from Delphi and from Daulia meet. We have come so far in the play, and the sense of place has played no great part. Thebes (where we witness the action) and Delphi with the snowy peaks of Parnassus above it have between them provided the imagined poles of the play's world. Even the question "Where was Laios killed, at home, in the country or abroad?" was answered only by "away from Thebes, they said on a journey" (ll. 112–14). There has been one brief, puzzling reference to another mountain, Kithairon, from Teiresias. No more. But now the "three roads" in the wooded, narrow ravine and the mountainside, with its upland pastures and glens, its caves, rocks and forest, gradually take on a more palpable and increasingly powerful reality. Another *polis,* that of Corinth, in double relationship, to Delphi and to the mountain, enters the world of the play to extend its geography. As the matter of place gathers in substance, so the issue of Oedipus's personality is joined by, at times almost resolves itself into, another question: the question "where does Oedipus belong?" To what? Where must he go? To Corinth, returning to become king? Or to the forested mountainside where the chorus has already imagined the killer of Laios stumbling like a bull over the rocks? The issues of the *polis,* of Thebes and its plague, gradually fade and dissolve until by the end of the play they are quite lost sight of.

But all this lies in the future. All other questions (even the question of legitimacy: is he his father's son?) are swept aside as a gathering panic occupies Oedipus's mind at hearing mention of a place he remembers, the "three roads" where he once killed a man. If that man was Laios, Oedipus sees that he has cursed himself and severed himself from all relationship with his new-found community; that he is now living with the widow of his own victim, and that "the seer can see." The terrible thrust of that thought is mirrored in a new sparseness and precision in the language of Oedipus, as Stephen Spender has well observed: "The drama here lies in the pressure of the factual narrative on the language (as though Oedipus were reading from a book inscribed on his memory) unimpassioned by his usual hyperbole." These things work upon his mind, so that his earlier proud calmness and assurance fall away and are replaced by compulsive, almost obsessive fear. After Iokasta has taken him into the shelter and privacy of the house, she returns to report him unable to master fear; but now fear's plaything. He "lifts his mind high with every sort of hurt; unlike a man in his true mind, he does not judge new things by old, but is the toy of anyone who speaks, if he speaks fears." (ll. 914–17).

The concentration of attention at this point in the play on the state of Oedipus's mind is striking and unusual in Greek tragedy, and moreover teasing since this fear-ridden Oedipus, as we see him face his fear, does not lose that quickness of rationality which marked him hitherto. On the contrary, the swiftness with which one inference follows on another is undiminished, and it is still the habit of his mind to leap ahead in making connections, in picking on the link in the chain of reasoning that must be tested. Oedipus is still a reasoner and speaks the language of reason; it is as reasoner that he relentlessly pursues his cross-examination, first of the shepherd with the news from Corinth, then of the second shepherd who had once been in the household of Laios. But the language of Oedipus has one more surprise for us before all is out. His last, false inference is to guess that Iokasta's motive for trying to block discovery of the truth of his origins is fear of humiliation, fear that he should turn out to be the child of slaves. In reply to her plea to give over the search, he declares his determination to know his descent, and his own sense of himself now (ll. 1076–85): he is the "child of chance that gives good" and as her child will not be humiliated. "The months and time" are his "brothers" and have "seen him great as well as small."

Here is a new language and a new Oedipus for whom only Teiresias's riddling words earlier in the play ("This day will give you birth and will destroy you") have prepared us, an Oedipus whose vision of himself is as a being from another world of discourse than the now familiar political world of Thebes or of Corinth. Here is one who speaks a new language of abstraction and metaphor, a child of nature to whom the concerns of human society are something less than real. As he confronts the two shepherds and cross-questions them, still sharp and quick in inference, about their past encounters on the summer pastures of Kithairon, we see an Oedipus who is isolated now from the society of his *polis;* and we see him come face to face with another realm, figured in the scenery of that mountain encounter. We are the less surprised, I think, when the chorus in the song that precedes that final encounter, momentarily taking on the role of seer, imagine Oedipus as the child of some god by a mountain nymph, and Kithairon as his kindred and his nurse. That is an image of his severance from human society, in which, despite his assurance of belonging, he has played parts that have mockingly inverted the most basic of human relationships, the most fundamental laws of social existence, in unawareness murdering his father and producing children by his own mother, to reduce the language of kinship to meaninglessness in becoming his children's brother and his mother's husband.

The moment of discovery, which meant so much to Aristotle, is the moment of supreme emotional shock and of apparent revelation; but the revelation, I believe, is at most a partial apprehension of the truth. The chorus recoil from Oedipus's discovery in an instant reassessment of the whole meaning of human life, of human achievement and human existence. They burst out with a cry that reduces the whole sum of human life to nothing, and human achievement to a mocking, momentary apparition, a firework, an arrow that climbs and falls away and means nothing. They cry out their sense of utter, overwhelming alienation, and that of Thebes itself, from Oedipus: "If only, if only I had never set eyes on you, child of Laios." In the intensity of the moment we respond to that outcry, I take it, as though to a fundamental truth at last understood and accepted; but I am sure that it is not Sophocles' last word, and that the long final movement of the play demonstrates by how much it falls short of the wholeness of truth.

Before the re-entry of Oedipus himself, that final moment begins with the messenger speech, the one true messenger speech of the play. Not only in the rhetorical anguish of its introduction ("I think that not Istros nor yet Phasis could wash clean this house in cleansing, so many evils does it hide, so many now, instantly, will show to the light" [ll. 1227–29]), but in the language and structure of the speech itself, we respond to the full shock of Oedipus's passage from the world of the falsely imagined to the world of the real. Uniquely among the messenger speeches of surviving tragedy, this narrative avoids the use of direct speech; the utterance of Oedipus and Iokasta in the privacy of the house is throughout paraphrased, not spoken, by the messenger. The effect of this, and of the repeated use of abstraction and periphrasis, is to enact the messenger's refusal to become engaged, to play out the events of his narrative. The events pass in a kind of appalled silence. He holds them at a distance from himself and from us.

The Oedipus who now enters is one transformed by his blinding into another Teiresias, isolated, listening to his own voice sound in the air. His words and those of the chorus serve to underline the total alienation which divides him from them as citizens of Thebes; there are few things more coldly chilling in Greek tragedy than the absolute, icy factuality of the chorus' replies to Oedipus's agonised song of self-horror and self-loathing. "These things were exactly as you say" (l. 1336), "how I wish that I had not so much as known you" (l. 1348), and, most frighteningly, in answer to Oedipus's expressed wish to have been left to die, and his curse upon the shepherd who undid the shackles and rescued him: "I too would have wished that" (l. 1356). Oedipus is still the reasoner who argues that the act of self-blinding was a correct decision ("done best," l. 1369), but now, in his dark isolation, he moves in mind and memory away from Thebes, back through the places of his past experience before he came to Thebes—to Kithairon, to Corinth, and most vividly realised of all in his language, to the narrow, wooded valley where the three roads met. He ends with the human marriage that confounded every category of kinship, and the thought leads immediately to the request to be taken and placed "outside" (l. 1410), beyond the boundaries of human society.

Kreon's entry at this moment ironically echoes his first entry in the play: once more there is a political decision to be made, and once more the god's judgment to be sought, but now the decision is Kreon's and like Oedipus then, he will await the god's word and then act on it. This Kreon indeed possesses the same calm and reasonable assurance that was the mark of Oedipus in the opening scene, and like that Oedipus he has foreseen what must be done and has already sent for Oedipus's daughters for a last greeting and farewell. It is as if Oedipus, himself transformed into another Teiresias, is reborn in this new cool but humane Kreon. If humanity is the dominant motif in Kreon, in Oedipus it is acceptance of a kind of alienation. He asks to be sent back to the mountainside where his mother and father had determined he should die, to *his* mountain, to Kithairon. As Richmond Lattimore has pointed out, that is not a pointer to an actual future, beyond the play (the story ended otherwise), but it rounds out our final sense of Oedipus, and his of himself. He sees himself now as owed to another than Thebes, owed to wherever his fate lies. He parts from his children and goes, starkly, within the house, to wait for what the god may give.

What of the play's meaning? I have given an account of *King Oedipus* that concentrates attention on two things: on the mind and language of Oedipus, his sense of the world and of himself, and on the metaphoric significance of place in the play; and I have largely ignored issues of moral responsibility (whether Oedipus's or Apollo's) and the question of fate. That is because, it seems to me, that is how the play is. It has nothing to say about responsibility, almost nothing about fate, and seemingly very little about the workings of divinity. It has a lot to say, on the other hand, about the polarization of language and perception that divides Oedipus from Teiresias until the truth about himself is out, and Kreon from Oedipus until the end and beyond. It is not exactly an issue of humanity (Kreon and Oedipus are both human and humane) but of a comprehended order and of belonging. Kreon throughout fits snugly within the political order of Thebes; the rules of human society are natural to him, he speaks its language without strain and he understands its procedures. But Oedipus, for all his conviction of belonging, and of mastery of political power and social observance, is an alien; he does not belong and his not belonging is figured in the contradictions of his human relationships. He *is* Laios's son (not Polybus's), but it is Laios he kills; he turns his back on kinship in Corinth, but only to stumble into incest and death of kindred in Thebes.

These contradictions are given a metaphoric structure, are mapped, as it were, onto our experience of Oedipus by the oppositions of place within the play. Thebes and Corinth, Delphi, the crossing of the three roads and the mountainside of Kithairon come to stand for opposed worlds, realms of human and divine intelligibility. In the world of men Oedipus's story makes no sense; it confounds all understanding, outrages all norms, renders ludicrous the language of society, but in the world of the gods it can be foreseen and spoken, by Apollo at Delphi and by Teiresias, who being blind to the world of men speaks the language of the gods, the "unspeakable" of line 301.

Apollo's presence in the play presents a paradox. His participation in Oedipus's experience is undeniable; it would pass all limits of a reasonable suspension of belief to doubt that, and we have Iokasta's realisation to bring it home to us. And yet, as I have said, Apollo is not seen to act on the human stage of the play at all, and it requires us to press the text of Sophocles' drama beyond conviction to be sure we have detected his hand in the precise guidance of what occurs. The sense of an alien power, in this play, lies not in the recognisable actions of divinity, but in our sense of the coexistence of two worlds and in our coming to the realisation that in passing between them, in crossing the boundary that separates men from the gods, Oedipus at the end is cut off from men, maimed and made desolate, by his contact with divinity.

I would like to take a little further this matter of divinity in *King Oedipus*. We sense the presence of divinity, I have argued, through a tissue of paradox and contradiction in the play's language and action. In the astonishing play of coincidence, for example, the ironical economy of an action in which five (exposer of the infant Oedipus, recipient of the child, witness of Laios's killing, bringer of the news of Polybus's death, confidante of Iokasta) become two is sometimes (incredibly) put down to ineptitude or to the exigencies of Sophocles' theater; but it has that sickening "rightness" that Aristotle saw in the statue of Mitys falling on his killer (*Poetics* 9 1452a4ff.) and which speaks the incursion of divinity. Or again in the overtones of "belonging," Oedipus is "of Thebes," the son of its king, *eggenes Thebaios,* as Teiresias says of him (l. 452ff.), but he is also from "elsewhere," from the alien foreignness of mountain and of forking road. In this he is associated with Thebes itself and its citizens: they are "Kadmeians," and Kadmos was from elsewhere, from an alien world, but they are also "of the place," "sown men," autochthonous, of the soil itself. But more importantly, Oedipus's double-sidedness, the coexistence of contraries in his relationship to the community of men, associates him also with divinity. Dionysus too was of Thebes; in *Bacchae* its past king's grandson, its present king's cousin, but also from elsewhere, from Lydia or from Thrace. As in *King Oedipus* the point is reinforced by language and geography: Dionysus, like the Teiresias of *King Oedipus,* speaks the language of riddles and, like Oedipus, Pentheus can only respond uncomprehendingly (Dionysus: "You know not what your life is, nor what you do, nor what you are." Pentheus: "Pentheus, Agaue's son, my father Echion." [ll. 506–7]).

In the *Bacchae* too the polarities of space, of mountain against city, play a crucial part in defining the "otherness" of divinity, and when the man of the city, the political man, Pentheus, crosses the boundary which separates city from mountain he, too, is destroyed. Apollo again is "of Delos," but he too comes from elsewhere, from Lykia, from the far North, from somewhere other. Whatever these stories may say of historical "origins," they are perhaps more significant in what they say of divinity's essential, timeless double-sidedness. Gods such as Apollo and Dionysus are always both (and simultaneously) "of the place" and "from elsewhere," and this double-sidedness is not merely asserted in myths of arrival and return, but also enacted in ritual, in the processions which escort the god "back" to the sanctuary where he lives and has power, in the *eisagoge* of the Dionysia at Athens, in the stepterion at Delphi (described in Alcaeus fr. 307LP) or the Daphnephoria at Thebes (Photius *Bibl.* 321a–b).

It is this sense of Oedipus's belonging not wholly among men but also to an alien world, outside our understanding, mocking the order, the rules and values of human society, yet having its own coherence, its own logic of irony and coincidence—that is the central image of Sophocles' play. That other world is a world outside the limits of the human *polis,* penetrated by the marginal, by shepherds and by seers. This, and not the driving force of fate nor the issues of human or divine justice, is Sophocles' concern in *King Oedipus* and the true kernel of his religious statement.

To have dealt with those other issues, implicit though they might be taken to be in the story of Oedipus, would be to have written another play.

Chronology

497–496 B.C.E.	Sophocles born.
468	First victory in tragic competition.
443–42	Sophocles serves as Imperial Treasurer.
ca. 442	*Antigone* produced.
441–440	Sophocles serves as general.
440–430(ea.)	*Ajax* produced.
430–420(ea.)	*Trachiniae* produced.
429–425(ea.)	*Oedipus Rex* produced.
420(?)	*Electra* produced.
413	Sophocles serves as special state commissioner.
409	*Philoctetes* produced.
406–405	Sophocles dies.
401	*Oedipus at Colonus* produced posthumously.

Contributors

HAROLD BLOOM, Sterling Professor of the Humanities at Yale University, is the author of *The Anxiety of Influence, Poetry and Repression*, and many other volumes of literary criticism. His forthcoming study, *Freud: Transference and Authority*, attempts a full-scale reading of all of Freud's major writings. A MacArthur Prize Fellow, he is general editor of five series of literary criticism published by Chelsea House. During 1987–88, he served as Charles Eliot Norton Professor of Poetry at Harvard University.

BERNARD KNOX is Director of the Center for Hellenic Studies in Washington, D. C. He is the author of *Oedipus at Thebes* and *The Heroic Temper: Studies in Sophoclean Tragedy*.

JOHN JONES is a Merton College Fellow. He was Professor of Poetry at the University of Oxford from 1979 to 1984 and is the author of books on Wordsworth, Keats, and Dostoevsky.

E. R. DODDS was Regius Professor of Greek at the University of Oxford and the author of *The Greeks and the Irrational* and *The Ancient Concept of Progress*.

THOMAS GOULD is Professor of Classics at Yale University. He is the author of a book on Platonic love and a translation of the *Oedipus Rex*.

KARL REINHARDT was Professor of Classics at the University of Frankfurt until his death in 1958. He is the author of numerous studies on Greek philosophy and poetry.

J. P. VERNANT is Professor of Comparative Studies of Ancient Religions at the College de France and is the author of *Myth and Thought*

163

Among the Greeks, Myth and Society in Ancient Greece, and *The Origins of Greek Thought.*

CHARLES SEGAL is Professor of Classics at Brown University and the author of book-length studies on Sophocles, Euripides, Virgil, and Ovid.

JOHN GOULD is W. D. and H. O. Willis Professor of Greek at the University of Bristol and the author of *The Development of Plato's Ethics* and a variety of articles on Greek literature and ancient life.

Bibliography

Adkins, A. W. H. "Aristotle and the Best Kind of Greek Tragedy." *Classical Quarterly* 16 (1966): 78–102.

Bowra, C. M. *Sophoclean Tragedy*. Oxford: Clarendon Press, 1944.

Burton, R. W. B. *The Chorus in Sophocles' Tragedies*. Oxford: Clarendon Press, 1980.

Caldwell, Richard S. "The Blindness of Oedipus." *International Review of Psychoanalysis* 1 (1974): 207–18.

Cameron, Alister. *The Identity of Oedipus the King: Five Essays on the* Oedipus Tyrannos. New York: New York University Press, 1968.

Champlain, M. W. "*Oedipus Tyrannos* and the Problem of Knowledge." *Classical Journal* 64 (1968–69): 337–45.

Dawe, R. D. "Some Reflections on Ate and Hamartia." *Harvard Studies in Classical Philology* 72 (1967): 89–123.

Devereux, George. "Why Oedipus Killed Laius: A Note on the Complementary Oedipus Complex in Greek Drama." *International Journal of Psychoanalysis* 34 (1953): 132–41.

———. "Socio-Political Functions of the Oedipus Myth in Early Greece." *Psychoanalytic Quarterly* 32 (1963): 205–14.

———. "The Self-Blinding of Oedipus in Sophocles: *Oedipus Tyrannos*." *Journal of Hellenic Studies* 93 (1973): 36–49.

Dimock, G. "Oedipus: The Religious Issue." *Hudson Review* 21 (1968–69): 430–56.

Dyson, M. "Oracle, Edict and Curse in *Oedipus Tyrannos*." *Classical Quarterly* 23 (1973): 202–12.

Ehrenberg, Victor. *Sophocles and Pericles*. Oxford: Basil Blackwell, 1954.

Fergusson, F. *The Idea of a Theater*. Princeton: Princeton University Press, 1949, 13–41.

Fortes, M. *Oedipus and Job*. Cambridge: Cambridge University Press, 1959.

Gellie, George. *Sophocles: A Reading*. Melbourne: Melbourne University Press, 1972.

Giagrande, L. "Self-Knowledge." *Cahiers des Etudes Anciennes* 25 (1983): 61–67.

Golden, Lester M. "Freud's Oedipus: Its Mytho-Dramatic Basis." *American Imago* 24 (1967): 271–82.

Green, Andre. *The Tragic Effect: The Oedipus Complex*. Translated by A. Sheridan. Cambridge: Cambridge University Press, 1979.

Guthrie, Thomas. "Oedipus Myth in Ancient Greece." *Psychiatric Quarterly* 24 (1955): 543–54.

Harsh, P. W. "Implicit and Explicit in the *Oedipus Tyrannos.*" *American Journal of Philology* 79 (1958): 243–58.

Hathorn, R. Y. "The Existential Oedipus." *Classical Journal* 53 (1957–58): 223–30.

Hester, D. A. "Oedipus and Jonah." *Proceedings of the Cambridge Philological Society* 23 (1977): 32–64.

Hoey, Thomas. "On the Theme of Introversion in the *Oedipus Rex.*" *Classical Journal* 64 (1968–69): 296–99.

Howe, Thalia Philies. "Taboo in the Oedipus Theme." *Transactions of the American Philological Society* 93 (1962): 124–43.

Kamerbeek, J. C. *The Plays of Sophocles IV: The* Oedipus Tyrannos. (Leiden: Brill, 1967).

Kane, R. I. "Prophecy and Perception in the *Oedipus Rex.*" *Transactions of the American Philological Society* 105 (1975): 189–208.

Kaufmann, Walter. *Tragedy and Philosophy.* Garden City, N.Y.: Doubleday, 1969.

Keddie, J. N. "Justice in Sophocles' *Oedipus Tyrannos.*" *Antichthon* 10 (1976): 25–34.

Kirkwood, G. M. *A Study of Sophoclean Drama.* Ithaca, N.Y.: Cornell University Press, 1958.

Kitto, H. D. F. *Sophocles: Dramatist and Philosopher.* London: Oxford University Press, 1958.

————. *Poesis: Structure and Thought.* Berkeley: University of California Press, 1966.

Knox, Bernard. *Oedipus at Thebes.* New Haven: Yale University Press, 1957.

Lattimore, Richard. *The Poetry of Greek Tragedy.* Baltimore: The Johns Hopkins Press, 1958.

Lattimore, Steven. "Oedipus and Teiresias." *California Studies in Classical Antiquity* 8 (1975): 105–11.

Lefcowitz, B. "The Inviolate Grove." *Literature and Psychology* 17 (1967): 78–86.

Lenieks, V. "The Foot of Oidipous." *Classical World* 69 (1975): 35–44.

Lesky, Albin. *Greek Tragedy.* New York: Barnes & Noble Books, 1965.

Lloyd-Jones, H. *The Justice of Zeus.* Berkeley: University of California Press, 1971, 104–28.

McDevitt, A. S. "Dramatic Imagery in the Parodos of the *Oedipus Tyrannos.*" *Wiener Studien* 4 (1970): 28–38.

Margon, J. S. "Aristotle and the Irrational and Improbable Elements in *Oedipus Rex.*" *Classical World* 70 (1976): 249–55.

Musurillo, H. *The Light and the Darkness: Studies in the Dramatic Poetry of Sophocles.* (Leiden: Brill, 1967).

Owen, E. T. "Drama in Sophocles' *Oedipus Tyrannos.*" *University of Toronto Quarterly* 10 (1940–41): 47–58.

Paolucci, Anne. "The Oracles Are Dumb or Cheat: A Study of the Meaning of *Oedipus Rex.*" *Classical Journal* 58 (1963): 241–47.

Peradotto, John J. "Oedipus and Erischthonius." *Arethusa* 10 (1977): 85–101.

Rado, Charles. *"Oedipus the King:* An Interpretation." *Psychoanalytic Review* 43 (1956): 228–34.

Reik, Theodor. *Dogma and Compulsion: Psycho-analytic Studies of Religion and Myth.* New York: International Universities Press, 1951.

Rigsby, K. J. "Teiresias as Magus in *Oedipus Rex." Greek, Roman and Byzantine Studies* 17 (1976): 109–14.

Rosenmeyer, Thomas G. "The Wrath of Oedipus." *Phoenix* 6 (1952): 92–112.

Scodel, H. "Hybris in the Second Stasimon of the *Oedipus Rex." Classical Philology* 77 (1982): 214–23.

Seal, David. *Vision and Stagecraft in Sophocles.* Chicago: University of Chicago Press, 1982.

Segal, Charles. *Tragedy and Civilization.* Cambridge, Mass.: Harvard University Press, 1981.

Sewall, Richard B. *The Vision of Tragedy.* New Haven: Yale University Press, 1959, 25–43.

Stewart, Harold. "Jocasta's Crimes." *International Journal of Psychoanalysis* 42 (1961): 424–30.

Stinton, T. C. W. "Hamartia in Aristotle and Greek Tragedy." *Classical Quarterly* 25 (1975): 221–54.

Thass-Thienemann, Theodore. "Oedipus-Identity-Knowledge" Part 2. *Subconscious Language.* New York: Washington Square Press, Inc., 1967.

Van der Sterren, H. A. "The *King Oedipus* of Sophocles." *International Journal of Psychoanalysis* 33 (1952): 343–50.

Vellacott, Philip. *Sophocles and Oedipus: A Study of the* Oedipus Tyrannos. (London: Macmillan Press, 1971).

Vernant, Jean-Pierre. "From Oedipus to Periander: Lameness, Tyranny, Incest in Legend and History." *Arethusa* 15 (1982): 19–38.

Vickers, Brian. *Towards Greek Tragedy.* London: Longman Ltd., 1973.

Wachtel, A. "On Analogical Action." *Journal of Aesthetics and Art Criticism* 22 (1963): 153–59.

Waldock, A. J. A. *Sophocles the Dramatist.* Cambridge: Cambridge University Press, 1951.

Weil, H. S. "Oedipus Rex: The Oracles and the Action." *Texas Studies in Literature and Language* 10 (1968): 337–48.

Whitman, Cedric H. *Sophocles: A Study of Heroic Humanism.* Cambridge, Mass.: Harvard University Press, 1951.

Winnington-Ingram, R. R. *Sophocles: An Interpretation.* Cambridge: Cambridge University Press, 1980.

Acknowledgments

"Sophocles' *Oedipus*" by Bernard Knox from *Tragic Themes in Western Literature*, edited by Cleanth Brooks, © 1955 by Yale University. Reprinted by permission of Yale University Press.

"Action and Actors" by John Jones from *On Aristotle and Greek Tragedy* by John Jones, © 1962 by John Jones. Reprinted by permission of the author and Chatto & Windus, Ltd.

"On Misunderstanding the *Oedipus Rex*" by E. R. Dodds from *Greece and Rome* 13, no. 1 (April 1966), © 1966 by Oxford University Press. Reprinted by permission of Oxford University Press.

"The Innocence of Oedipus: The Philosophers on *Oedipus the King*" by Thomas Gould from *Arion* 5, no. 4 (Winter 1966), © 1966 by the Trustees of Boston University. Reprinted by permission.

"Illusion and Truth in *Oedipus Tyrannus*" (Originally entitled "Oedipus Tyrannus") by Karl Reinhardt from *Sophocles* by Karl Reinhardt, © 1979 in this translation by Basil Blackwell. Reprinted by permission of Basil Blackwell Limited, Oxford.

"Ambiguity and Reversal: On the Enigmatic Structure of *Oedipus Rex*" by J. P. Vernant from *Tragedy and Myth in Ancient Greece* by J. P. Vernant, © 1981 this translation by The Harvester Press, Ltd. Reprinted by permission of The Harvester Press Ltd./Wheatsheaf Books Ltd. and The Humanities Press International, Inc., Atlantic Highlands, N.J.

"The Music of the Sphinx: The Problem of Language in *Oedipus Tyrannus*" by Charles Segal from *Contemporary Literary Hermeneutics and Interpretations of Classic Texts,* edited by Stephen Kresic, © 1981 by the University of Ottawa Press. Reprinted by permission of the University of Ottawa Press.

"The Language of Oedipus" by John Gould, © 1987 by John Gould. Published for the first time in this volume. Printed by permission.

Index

171